HBR Guide to
Managing
Strategic
Initiatives

Harvard Business Review Guides

Arm yourself with the advice you need to succeed on the job, from the most trusted brand in business. Packed with how-to essentials from leading experts, the HBR Guides provide smart answers to your most pressing work challenges.

The titles include:

HBR Guide for Women at Work

HBR Guide to Being More Productive

HBR Guide to Better Business Writing

HBR Guide to Building Your Business Case

HBR Guide to Buying a Small Business

HBR Guide to Changing Your Career

HBR Guide to Coaching Employees

HBR Guide to Data Analytics Basics for Managers

HBR Guide to Dealing with Conflict

HBR Guide to Delivering Effective Feedback

HBR Guide to Emotional Intelligence

HBR Guide to Finance Basics for Managers

HBR Guide to Getting the Mentoring You Need

HBR Guide to Getting the Right Work Done

HBR Guide to Leading Teams

HBR Guide to Making Better Decisions

HBR Guide to Making Every Meeting Matter

HBR Guide to Managing Strategic Initiatives

HBR Guide to Managing Stress at Work

HBR Guide to
Managing Strategic Initiatives

HARVARD BUSINESS REVIEW PRESS

Boston, Massachusetts

Copyright 2020 Harvard Business School Publishing Corporation

Printed in the United States of America

10 9 8 7 6 5 4 3 2 1

The web addresses referenced in this book were live and correct at the time of the book's publication but may be subject to change.

Library of Congress Cataloging-in-Publication Data

Title: HBR guide to managing strategic initiatives.
Other titles: Harvard Business Review guide to managing strategic initiatives | Harvard business review guides.
Description: Boston, Massachusetts : Harvard Business Review Press, [2020] | Series: Harvard Business Review guides | Includes index.
Identifiers: LCCN 2019035457 | ISBN 9781633698185 (paperback) | ISBN 9781633698192 (ebook)
Subjects: LCSH: Project management. | Strategic planning. | Business planning. | Success in business. | Leadership.
Classification: LCC HD69.P75 H393 2020 | DDC 658.4/04—dc23
LC record available at https://lccn.loc.gov/2019035457

ISBN: 978-1-63369-818-5
eISBN: 978-1-63369-819-2

The paper used in this publication meets the requirements of the American National Standard for Permanence of Paper for Publications and Documents in Libraries and Archives Z39.48-1992.

What You'll Learn

Strategic initiatives are the key projects and programs that will transform your company from what it is now into what it needs to be. But choosing the right strategic initiatives and running them effectively can be a serious challenge for new managers and seasoned leaders alike.

It begins with deciding which initiatives to pursue among many worthy possibilities. Then you have to navigate the politics of approvals and allocating resources. Once a project is up and running, you need to keep it on track and aligned with your company's strategy. You may have to overcome in-house resistance to keep things from backsliding—especially if your initiative brings about change for your team or the organization.

Also keep in mind that no initiative exists in isolation. It's not enough just to manage each project the right way; you need to know how to oversee multiple initiatives and to understand how *all* of your company's initiatives are working together to move your strategy forward.

Whether you're pitching your first signature project or overseeing an established portfolio of initiatives, this book will provide you with the tools, tips, and advice you need to run them effectively, whether within your team or across the company. You'll learn how to:

- Win—and keep—support for your new idea

- Move rapidly from approval to implementation

- Assemble transformative, high-performing initiative teams

- Stay on schedule and within budget

- Avoid losing momentum once you're up and running

- Maintain the confidence of your project's sponsors and stakeholders

- Avoid initiative overload by killing programs that aren't meeting business needs

- Manage multiple initiatives as a portfolio, and keep them all aligned with your company's strategy

Contents

Contents

SECTION FOUR

Maintaining Momentum and Overcoming Challenges

SECTION FIVE

Keeping Strategy and Execution Aligned

Putting Strategy into Action

You have an exciting day ahead. At 9:00 you're leading a cross-department brainstorming session to generate new ideas for what your company needs to do to get ahead of regulatory changes that are coming to your industry. At 10:00 you're sitting in on a bimonthly group that reviews the progress of the dozen innovation projects your department is running. And at 1:00, you'll be presenting the business case to your unit leaders to spearhead a pilot program to make your company culture more friendly to working parents.

All three of these are examples of strategic initiatives, and your schedule is full of them. Each meeting is with a different team that has been assembled specifically for this task. Perhaps none of these are your "day job." As a manager, you could be playing any role in an initiative on any given day. You might be championing your employee's idea across your department or pitching your own proposal to senior executives. You might be a team member or a team leader on a cross-functional project. You might be the one fighting for more funding for a program or part of the committee that decides whether a program should be cut.

Managing initiatives requires you to keep the big picture and the little details in your head at the same time, thinking like a project manager one minute and a CEO the next. To manage initiatives successfully, you need to learn how to choose them, launch them, sustain them, and shut them down if they're no longer effective. Whether you're a manager pitching your first signature program or an executive overseeing an established project portfolio, this book will provide you with the tools, tips, and practical advice you need to run initiatives effectively and put your company's strategy into action.

What Is a Strategic Initiative?

An initiative is a project or program outside a company's routine operational activities that is meant to help the company achieve its strategy. Initiatives include such things as instituting change, creating a capability, improving performance, streamlining a process, balancing the needs of current economic conditions with the future, raising customer satisfaction, increasing employee retention, or ensuring regulatory compliance.

Initiatives follow a number of common steps at any organization, though the formal structure around each step will differ based on the size and culture of your company.

- **Idea generation.** Ideas at your company might come directly from executives or may be solicited from employees. Inspiration may come via group brainstorms or solitary eureka moments. They may spread through formal channels or through hallway chats. No matter how the ideas for initiatives come about, for them to progress, they need a shepherd to tend them and push them forward toward implementation.

- **Building a business case and presentation to decision makers.** This step consists of the legwork in fleshing out the idea, collecting needed data, running the numbers, getting feedback from stakeholders, winning over supporters, and pitching to decision makers.

- **Evaluation, approval, and prioritization.** Your organization should have a clear and fair process for evaluating initiative proposals and then accepting or rejecting them. Once they're approved, they are prioritized or put into classes or categories to make clear which are most and least critical to the company.

- **Launch, implementation, and learning.** The prework is done, and the initiative has the green light—act. Secure the funding you need and assemble your all-star team. The initiative is now a project to be managed effectively and monitored until it is showing the results you've promised. And whether or not the initiative is a hands-down success or a disappointment, you need to capture what you've learned throughout the process and communicate it to stakeholders.

These steps may all seem simple enough, but initiatives don't exist in isolation. Two more ongoing processes should be taking place throughout an initiative's life cycle:

- **Review of the company's portfolio of initiatives.**
  Effective organizations should frequently look at *all* of the initiatives that are happening in the company (or unit, or department) together, to make sure they are reaching milestones, continuing to meet business needs, and are reprioritized accordingly. Are any initiatives redundant? Are any more valuable in aggregate than they would be in isolation? Underperforming initiatives should be identified, their given assistance or cut. Resources are limited, and not every strategically worthy project can be funded—initiatives that aren't meeting business needs should be killed to make way for others.

- **Alignment of strategy and execution.** "Alignment" isn't a static characteristic or a box to be checked before an initiative is approved—it's part of an ongoing process that will ensure your projects continue to further strategic goals in a changing environment, perhaps quarters or years after launch. Initiatives are the strongest tools your organization has to execute its strategy. You can't ensure that your initiatives are actually supporting your company's strategy unless you are frequently confirming that there's no gap between strategy and execution.

This framework applies to just about any initiative in any industry. Now that you have the basics down, let's dive into the challenges.

Why Is Managing Initiatives So Difficult?

Leading a strategic initiative requires all of the management skills you use in your day-to-day work, but brings additional challenges: navigating the office politics of gaining approval and getting funded, keeping support of your project from crumbling, overcoming resistance to change, leading without formal authority, building up teams quickly, course-correcting on the fly, and making the changes that you've pioneered stick—just to name a few. Plus add in the stress of knowing that having your name on a successful initiative—or a flop—could have a big effect on your career track.

Meanwhile, many organizations don't make it easy for their managers. Companies of all kinds struggle with their strategic initiatives. Some put up too many bureaucratic obstacles to allow initiatives to get off the ground, while others launch too many and spread their resources too thin. Initiatives proceed to implementation without business cases or success metrics. Band-Aid initiatives and unfunded mandates proliferate. Inadequate portfolio review allows pet projects and underperforming initiatives to go on for too long, spreading resources thin and starving more-worthy projects. The financial costs to the company and the human toll in the form of frustration, burnout, and turnover can be severe.

It doesn't have to be this way. The practices covered in this book can help you and your company find greater success as you manage initiatives, while using processes that are fair, sustainable, and effective.

What This Book Will Do

The *HBR Guide to Managing Strategic Initiatives* provides you with the knowledge, tips, and tools you need whether you are leading an initiative, championing your employee's project, overseeing an initiative portfolio, or just have a great idea to push your company's strategy forward. The five sections in this book will give you a good idea where to start. You can begin at section one if you're at an early stage, or jump in later if your initiative is already off the ground.

From idea to pitch

This section focuses on the work you need to do to when you have a great idea for an initiative, whether or not your company has a formal approval process. It begins with an overview on winning support for your project, covering how to get people on board, how to work with a champion on the review committee, how to secure funding, and what to do if your idea doesn't take off. Chapter 2 covers mistakes to avoid in order to prevent the disappearance of support for your initiative. The third article in the section explains what you should do next after you've presented the case for your initiative to decision makers—whether you've heard yes, no, or something in between.

Evaluating and prioritizing a portfolio of initiatives

Initiatives need to be evaluated both on their own merits and on how they contribute to the company's strategy—and even if you're not the one making the call on whether a proposal makes the cut, it's important that you know how and why higher-ups in your organization are making these decisions. Chapter 4 describes a rigorous and rational process of evaluating which projects to implement that can be used at the department or unit level, or across the company. Next, "A Better Way to Set Strategic Priorities" shows a fair, transparent way to deal with trade-offs when resources become limited. "Too Many Projects" explores how initiative overload can lead to poor-quality work and burnout, and includes a list of questions to ask before you launch any initiative. And chapters 7 and 8 explore best practices for reviewing your company's portfolio of initiatives, monitoring each project actively for health and strategic fit, and thinking like an investment manager to keep the portfolio balanced and diversified.

Launching and implementing initiatives

Once you have the go-ahead, you want to get up to speed quickly and avoid stumbling when moving into the implementation stage. "New Project? Don't Analyze—Act" teaches you to embrace lessons from serial entrepreneurs—to act, learn, and build fast to get your initiative off the ground. Chapter 10 is a five-step refresher on project management to make sure your team is staying on top of deadlines, keeping stakeholders informed, and managing changes to the initial plan. Next, "Building a Transformative Team" will help you look at whether you have the right mix of players to thrive in uncertainty. Chapter 12 covers how to bring together experts to solve problems they may be encountering for the first and only time, sharing their learnings with your company *while* they're executing. Finally, chapter 13 describes how to use the technique of *rapid-results initiatives* to break large, long-term initiatives into short-term projects distributed among numerous teams.

Maintaining momentum and overcoming challenges

Many initiatives will hit common roadblocks. Teams fail to gel, critical members are lost, early predictions prove wrong, attention wanders amid competing initiatives, underperforming programs limp along, champions lose their attention. This section will help you deal with these challenges to keep initiatives moving forward successfully. Chapter 14 will aid you in re-centering yourself and your team if your project isn't finding its groove in the execution stage. "Learning in the Thick of It" shows how before-action reviews and after-action reviews can help you stay on track and sense when change is needed. The next two chapters explain how to avoid problems when handing off a project from one team to another and provide techniques leaders can use to prevent process improvements from backsliding when the *next* change initiative comes. Finally, since healthy initiative portfolio management means that not every initiative that is started will be completed, the last article in the section shows how "exit champions" can ensure the right projects are killed to make room for more-worthy investments.

Keeping strategy and execution aligned

While strategic alignment might not seem as urgent as the deadline-driven, day-to-day challenges of implementation, ignore it at your own risk. If your project is misaligned with your company's strategy, it may be in danger of being cut at any moment. And if your company's portfolio of initiatives is full of scattershot projects that aren't advancing the strategy, your whole company could be in trouble soon. You can read the articles in this section any time—they are equally relevant at any stage of an initiative. Chapter 19 discusses four tensions that characterize any execution effort and provides guidance on how to navigate them. The next chapter demonstrates how the best companies close the strategy-to-execution gap by using agile, test-and-learn approaches. Finally, "Your Strategy Has to Be Flexible—But So Does Your Execution" explores the dangers of thinking about strategy and execution as two separate tasks.

Managing initiatives will never be simple—that's why leaders who run them effectively will see themselves rising through the ranks, and organizations that oversee a healthy portfolio of initiatives will surpass their competitors. The advice in this book can ease the challenges, help you avoid common pitfalls, and help you move your company and your career forward. You'll learn to lead projects and navigate uncertainty with greater confidence, overcome roadblocks, avoid initiative overload, and put your company's strategy into action. Let's get started.

From Idea to Pitch

CHAPTER 1

A Guide to Winning Support for Your New Idea or Project

by Rebecca Knight

You've got an idea for something that will improve your company's bottom line or make it a better place to work. Nice going. Now for the hard part: How do you get people on board? How do you get funding? And what should you do if your idea doesn't catch on?

What the Experts Say

In an ideal world, you'd come up with a genius new idea and tell your coworkers about it, and they'd immediately

Adapted from content posted on hbr.org, June 19, 2015 (product #H025YR).

grasp its brilliance. Your boss would love it—and you!—and give you the resources you need to execute it. But that's not reality. "It's very hard to start a new initiative," says John Butman, author of *Breaking Out: How to Build Influence in a World of Competing Ideas.* "It's hard to get people to listen to your idea, to understand your idea, and to take action." It may be difficult, but it's also a vital skill to master. "Organizations need to keep changing, adapting, and innovating," he says. "If they don't, they stagnate and disappear." But it's not only the success of your company that's at stake, says Susan Ashford, professor of management and organization at the University of Michigan's Ross School of Business. The ability to get new initiatives off the ground is also critical to your career. "You want to stand out, be visible, and get noticed as a leader," she says. "And one of the ways to do this is by suggesting change ideas and implementing them." Here are some pointers on how to get your idea moving.

Understand what's motivating you

Before you breathe a word about your idea to a colleague, you must "think through your motives," advises Butman. Ask yourself two questions: Why am I doing this? And what do I hope to accomplish? "You need to be able to express your motives" in a way that's relatable and compelling to others, says Butman. "If the initiative seems like something that will only make you more successful, give you more exposure, or help you get a better job," people will be skeptical. "It needs to benefit more than just you. Otherwise you're going to run into trouble."

Think small

Next, you need to pinpoint "your idea by making it as specific and small as it can possibly be," Butman says. Pick precisely where you want to focus. If your new initiative involves, say, improving employee health, zero in on a particular goal, such as decreasing employees' back pain or helping workers quit smoking. This exercise helps you "articulate the issue" you're trying to address, and explain why your initiative "offers a possible solution," says Ashford. Your colleagues are more likely to respond to specific initiatives rather than lofty, ambiguous goals.

Gather feedback

Test the waters for your idea by making frequent use of what Butman refers to as "the cocktail party test." When you find yourself with colleagues who might be interested in your initiative—whether they are close coworkers or people from an entirely different department or division—broach your idea in an informal way. "Present your idea by saying something like, 'I've been thinking about this,' or 'What would you think of this?'" suggests Butman. Then, listen carefully to what people tell you. "You want questions. You want opposing viewpoints. You want pushback," he says. The goal is to get to a place where no matter what anybody throws at you, you have a response. "Be sure to integrate their feedback into your game plan," adds Ashford. "It's a process of iteration and figuring out" what works.

Shape your story for the audience

Strategize how you'll sell your initiative to different groups of colleagues and higher-ups. "Think about the language you'll use for each of your audiences," says Ashford. "You need to be seen as credible" when you're talking about the financial implications of your initiative to the finance group, for instance. "You need to be able to talk about your idea succinctly and vividly and in a solutions-oriented way," she adds. After all, "if you're in an elevator with a decision maker, you have only so much time to talk and you can't very well shoot your PowerPoint slides up on the walls." And bear in mind that "everyone has different learning styles," says Butman. "You can't expect to write a white paper and slap it on people's desks." For this reason, it's important to vary your messaging with "something written, something spoken, something visual, and perhaps even tangible." Butman recommends using a personal story to provide context. "Give people some idea of how you came up with the idea and why it's meaningful to you as a human being." Ashford concurs. Your presentation and pitch "should not be just a bunch of charts and graphs; it should have visual appeal," she says.

Sell, sell, sell

Selling your idea is "not a singular event—it's a campaign," according to Ashford. "You need to do a lot of watercooler talk with different kinds of people." Getting people to nod their heads in agreement is the first step, but to spark excitement and secure funding you need to inspire. "You want to trigger people's emotions as well as their rational selves," she says. Your aim is to "reduce resistance, bring people on board, and band allies and resources together." You should be "closing the deal all the time," adds Butman. "When you talk about it, you want people getting a little bit more of the idea and signing on to it a little bit more each time." The goal, he says, is "internal virality" through "incremental agreement." One word to the wise: When you're trying to get others on board, don't use the word *new*. "That's the language of marketing," says Butman. Colleagues need to be able to understand your idea in the context of the company's past measures. "People often think their initiative has to be newer than new, but really it should be between 80% and 90% old—not radically new, but incrementally so."

Propose a pilot

Ashford suggests proposing a trial run. It could be in the spirit of "Let's not worry about making this change wholesale—let's try a pilot," she says. "It reduces the perceived risk" of implementing something big and new. Pilots "give people a chance to test out" the idea. "And they can also create data that changes minds." If you don't have the power to allocate budget to a pilot, you need to sell harder to those who do. "Organizations have limited time, attention, and money," says Ashford. Don't lose sight of the fact that you're constantly "competing against other people's ideas" and other people's doggedness. "If you and your allies really care about something, you need to sell it"; a pilot is often a cost-effective way to do it.

Don't get discouraged

Even when it seems you're constantly running into road-blocks and your initiative may never get off the ground, don't be deterred. "Sometimes an idea catches on right away, and sometimes it takes decades for it to take hold," says Butman. Persistence is key. But this does not mean persistence at all costs. Make sure you're incorporating people's feedback—both the good ideas and the potential sticking points—into your pitch. "Give up your desire for credit and control, and let people help you," says Butman. It all gets back to your motives, says Ashford. "You need to care about the idea, not getting credit for the idea," she says. "Think about what's good for all, not just what will let you shine. Trust the universe" that you will get credit when it's due. (See the sidebar "Who Will Have Your Back?")

Principles to Remember

Do

- Make your idea as specific as possible and emphasize how it offers a clear solution to a targeted problem.

- Adapt your sales pitch to the audience.

- Suggest a pilot of your plan—trials are less risky and less expensive.

Don't

- Insist on getting credit for the initiative—colleagues are less likely to support your idea if they sense you're only in it for yourself.

- Forget to solicit feedback from your colleagues.

- Give up if your idea doesn't immediately gain traction—change sometimes takes longer than you'd like.

Case Study: Use a Relatable Story to Sell Your Idea; Be Patient with Implementation

Julie Wittes Schlack, SVP of Innovation and Design at C Space, the global consulting company, knew that her company needed to streamline its client services, but she wasn't sure how to get the idea off the ground. "We had all these codified processes that we were doing just because that's the way we had always worked," she says.

Then, one day, when Julie and C Space's management team were at the company's annual off-site retreat, they had a moment of clarity. During one of the sessions, they read a case study about a hotel chain that trimmed labor and production costs by ceasing to launder guest sheets every day. It was a story that Julie and her team immediately related to.

"It was the first hotel chain to ask, is [every day] linen changing necessary?" says Julie. "Linen changing became a great metaphor for our own cumbersome and obsolete processes."

WHO WILL HAVE YOUR BACK?

by Raymond Sheen and Amy Gallo

Finding a champion on the review committee—or one who's close to it—will help you get a fair review, because she will lobby on behalf of your case. But how do you find a project champion?

Look at each member of the review committee: Whose goals and concerns will your project address most directly? That person is a potential champion. Reach out and ask what her department is trying to achieve in the coming year. Get a sense of what big projects are under way and which need more support. Explain how your initiative can help fill in gaps or address trouble spots. This is a time when your personal network will pay dividends. Work with people you know in that department or division to clarify the problem or business need that your project will address. Ask them specifically what the champion will care most about and how to address those concerns. Then, ask your

When Julie and the other senior leaders returned to the office, they worked to get other employees on board with the initiative to restructure client services—which accounted for three-fourths of the organization. They began by sharing the hotel story in meetings and in casual conversation. "People internalized the idea," says Julie, adding that from then on employees used "Are we

contacts to introduce you to the potential champion or to set up a meeting so you can clarify the need and explain your ideas. Even if you've never met the potential champion, you're more likely to get her ear since you're working on a problem that affects her division. If she is interested, ask her to review your business case when it's ready and champion it within the review committee. You'll also want to keep her informed and use her as a sounding board along the way.

Of course, having someone influential on your side does little good if you don't have a strong case that meets a business need and well-thought-out financials. If those elements are missing, even a powerful champion can't help you. So now that you've won over one person, it's time to tailor your pitch to meet the objectives of the organization and the broader committee.

Adapted from *HBR Guide to Building Your Business Case* (product #15038E), by Raymond Sheen with Amy Gallo, Harvard Business Review Press, 2015.

just linen changing?" to refer to processes that were not critical to the organization. "It was a shorthand and an easy way for people to talk about [the restructuring] as they were going about their daily tasks. Is this [process] necessary? Is this desirable?"

They had buy-in from employees, but when it came to implementing the initiative and eliminating certain

processes, Julie received some pushback. To deal with it, Julie diagrammed the current system to show how many different people and departments were involved in each process. "It became easier for others to see where there was overhead and get aligned on [where we could cut back]," she says.

Restructuring client services was a six-month process, but ultimately her employees embraced the initiative because it saved them time and it saved the company money. "They saw what was necessary and what was adding value," she says.

Rebecca Knight is a freelance journalist in Boston and a lecturer at Wesleyan University. Her work has been published in the *New York Times, USA Today,* and the *Financial Times.*

CHAPTER 2

How to Keep Support for Your Project from Evaporating

by Allison Rimm

Even years later, I still consider it my biggest professional failure: A companywide employee training program that I'd developed and put through several rounds of vetting was shot down at the last minute. It was a painful surprise, and it changed the way I've sought support for new initiatives ever since.

As hospitals increasingly migrate their medical records from paper files to digital media, their employees

---

Adapted from content posted on hbr.org, August 10, 2015 (product #H028WC).

face the challenge of making the information readily accessible to providers while adequately protecting patients' privacy. At my hospital, I was a senior vice president with a long track record of establishing successful programs, and I had oversight responsibility for my hospital's IT and health information departments.

To make sure our 23,000+ employees were up to date on the industry rules, policies, and procedures they were legally required to be familiar with, my department heads and I created a robust training program. We went well beyond the minimum that the law required, creating a curriculum rooted in industry best practices. We could have just printed out a thick informational packet to give to each employee, but we knew the training program had a much greater chance of being effective. And we gave the program a catchy name to top it off.

From the outset, I understood the training program would require the support of the entire senior management team, as they would have to direct their departments to complete the training and document that they had done so. As our multidisciplinary team developed the curriculum, I provided regular updates to my colleagues and asked for their input throughout the process. With each vetting, they indicated their support of the initiative. So when the pushback finally happened, I never saw it coming.

Timing is everything. When the final vote on the training program arrived, another vice president, who had been supportive of the program, had just come from a meeting where his pet project was shot down. He was livid about his defeat and was not in the mood to approve my program. In fact, he made such an angry speech that

a few others in the room weren't up to arguing with him. My initiative was tabled.

In hindsight, I had made two mistakes. In the highly regulated world of health care, training programs are introduced continuously with little fanfare. I gave my program a catchy name to make what was, frankly, a tedious chore a little more inviting to the many people who would have to complete it. Giving mine a sexy name made it sound like a full-blown program that would consume significant resources, raising its profile more than was warranted.

The second mistake was assuming that when my colleagues smiled and nodded every time I presented the details, they would continue their support no matter what was happening outside the conference room. My angry colleague being so riled up was not the time to remind him that the training met a critical need and was something we had to pursue.

Of course, angry outburst aside, the work still needed to be done. So, I waited a few weeks and went to visit my disappointed colleague once he'd had a chance to cool off. I reminded him that it was important for this program to go forward, and I asked him what it would take to get him behind the effort. We negotiated a few points and came up with a plan we could both support. I then asked him to present our changes at the next senior management meeting so it would be clear to everyone in the room that he was back on board. That time, the vote carried.

Nearly a decade later, I'm actually grateful to him for teaching me a valuable lesson. I had been so sure of the strength of my professional relationships that I'd just assumed everyone would remain consistent and true to their word, regardless of what it would cost them in an unforeseeable situation such as the one we found ourselves in that day.

As a result of this experience, when I'm developing a project now, I ask for and record votes at every vetting and make those records available for review. That way, if there is ever a disagreement about the status of one of my projects, there is a clear record of everyone's position, making it more difficult for people to change their stance in the heat of the moment. I also log undecided votes when people haven't made up their minds yet, but I've found that people usually form opinions about new projects pretty quickly. If I'd had documentation of everyone's support for the training program, their positions would have been clear, so there would have been no need for me to go up against our angry colleague.

Second, I learned to wait until something is actually approved to give it an eye-catching name and brand it as a stand-alone program. When the training was finally approved a few weeks later, we gave it a new name—the result of a contest among the employees who would have to take it—which truly helped people understand what needed to be done and how to do it. But naming a program too early runs the risk of creating a sense among your teammates, who may be promoting their own initiatives, that there are winners and losers.

Most of us work in environments where there are many initiatives competing for limited resources of budgets, time, and attention. Sobered by my surprising upset, I've taken pains to formalize the vetting process and not rely on friendships and collegial alliances. In fact, the higher the stakes, the more formal the process I use. Not all industries may need a process as formal as mine, but it's important to figure out the best way to get projects approved where you work.

Here's an example of how I use this process to facilitate budget negotiations. To prioritize the requests for expensive IT initiatives whose demands far exceeded the resources available each year, I created a multidisciplinary senior-level steering committee to evaluate various initiatives and sort them by order of strategic and operational importance. Votes were all documented. When I entered into budget negotiations with the other SVPs, I was armed with a record of who supported each initiative. The relevant SVPs either sat on the steering committee or were represented. In this way, we avoided the seriously unpleasant task of making the case for each initiative in the heat of the budget battle. The work of the steering committee allowed a full vetting in a neutral setting—which is exactly what the budget room is not.

I'm happy to report that since adopting these two practices, I've never endured the same kind of defeat, even when the stakes have been high. Maybe that experience wasn't such a failure after all.

———————

Allison Rimm is a management consultant, speaker, and executive coach devoted to nurturing a positive, productive workplace. She is the former senior vice president for strategic planning and information management at Massachusetts General Hospital and best-selling author of *The Joy of Strategy: A Business Plan for Life*.

CHAPTER 3

You've Pitched Your Initiative— What's Next?

by Raymond Sheen with Amy Gallo

After you've presented the business case for your initiative, you may be popping a bottle of bubbly, walking despondently back to your desk, or pulling your hair out because you have to create and present a case all over again.

But the work is not over. Even if the decision makers said no, there are steps you can and should take. If you got a yes, it's time to begin implementing your project.

Adapted from *HBR Guide to Building Your Business Case* (product #15038E), by Raymond Sheen with Amy Gallo, Harvard Business Review Press, 2015, pp. 109–117.

If You Heard "No, the Project Isn't a Priority"

First off, don't despair if your project isn't approved. Although it may feel like failure to hear "no," keep in mind that you've contributed to the success of the company by helping it identify that the project wasn't a worthwhile investment. The real purpose of a business case is not to necessarily win approval for your proposal, but to provide enough information so the committee can make an informed decision.

But don't just accept the "no" by saying thank-you and walking away. Instead, always ask "Why?" If you know precisely why the decision makers rejected the case, then you'll be able to follow up appropriately. Ask this question in the meeting or in a subsequent email. Don't pick a fight or try to use the response to change the outcome, but seek to understand their reasoning. You might say, "Thanks for letting me know about your decision. I'd love any feedback you have on why the project wasn't approved."

The reviewers may have passed on your project for any of several reasons. For example, they might tell you that the project doesn't align with the company strategy. In this case, let it die. Any project that doesn't fit with the company's imperatives should be rejected.

If they thought the project wasn't viable—that the approach you described wouldn't yield the results you promised—you can go back and address their concerns. Do you need more data to show why the approach works? Can you create a prototype that will assuage their worries? You might ask for a small amount of funding to run a quick pilot to prove the project can succeed.

If the higher-ups say no because there aren't enough resources, hold on to your case in the event that resources become available. That actually happened to me at GE. Partway through the year, corporate decided to give our business unit some additional funding to invest in strategic product development projects. Some market dynamics had changed, making our market segments more attractive than others. The product manager and I quickly dusted off several business cases that had not been funded due to lack of resources during the previous year's strategic planning process. In less than a month, projects were approved and teams were getting down to work. Staying in close touch with your project champion so that she can keep you apprised of any changes will help you prepare for such opportunities.

When you ask for the reasons behind the rejection, you have to hope you'll get an honest answer. In most cases, you will. It may not be direct—the CEO may not say to you, "We didn't think you could pull off the project"—but you'll likely be able to infer the reasons. Try to read between the lines. If you're still not sure, ask the project champion for her insight. Whatever response you get, don't argue with the logic or take it personally. That's not a way to win allies—or support—for this or future projects.

If You Heard "We Can't Make a Decision Yet"

Having your proposal tabled is better than an outright no, but it's still disappointing. In most cases, you'll just have to trust that you built and presented a solid case and then wait and see what happens. Any additional measures you take will depend on the decision makers' rationale. Typically, it's for one of three reasons.

The case hasn't made the first cut

It could be that your case didn't make it into the "definite yes" pile. If the decision committee is reviewing multiple cases at once, it may divide proposals into yes, no, and maybe piles. At least you know your project is in the mix. There's no need to lobby for your case at this point, especially if your project champion is representing you to the decision makers.

The decision makers just haven't decided yet

Sometimes you've got a management team full of ditherers who are unable or unwilling to make decisions on the spot. They might want to hold off until they're behind closed doors to make the final call. Of course, your project is more likely to be approved if your proposal clarifies what's in it for each of the decision makers. While you wait, though, you may want to periodically work through your champion to be sure your idea is still in front of people and to check if there's anyone else's ear you should get.

Sometimes, the committee hasn't decided because they're waiting for the outcome of another decision that has farther-reaching impact. This happened to me once, when a project I'd proposed was hanging in the balance while we waited to find out if an acquisition that was in the works would be successful. If the acquisition went through, our project wouldn't be needed. If the deal didn't go through, our project would help fill a larger product development void.

The strategy is on hold

The third reason for tabling projects is that the strategy it supports is on hold or being reconceived. Use your internal network to stay abreast of where the strategy is going. Once you have that information, you'll have to tweak your case to reflect new goals, assumptions, or constraints. If your proposal focuses on U.S. customers, and your company has decided to focus more on European customers, for example, explore whether your idea could be carried out in the United Kingdom. Since you've done a good job preparing your business case, you'll easily be able to tweak it. This can be a great opportunity. Typically, senior leaders will want to do a project right away that aligns with the new imperatives to demonstrate support for the new strategy. With your carefully prepared plan, you could be first in line with a project that fits. Don't shoehorn your project into the new strategy, of course. If your case doesn't support it, don't make it.

Sometimes waiting for a final decision takes time—days, weeks, and even months. And the reason for the project—the pain point it's designed to address—likely isn't going away. There may not be a whole lot you can do, but look for opportunities to alleviate the pain a bit. If your case proposed a new system that would allow customer service representatives to respond more quickly to complaints, look for workarounds. Collaborate with the person heading up that department to see if he has any short-term ideas that will make things better.

While you're waiting, it's not a bad idea to find a simple, easy way to collect more information about the problem and its magnitude. Document what's happening so that when you have the opportunity to go back to the decision makers or to your project champion, you can say, "This problem hasn't gone away; in fact, it's gotten worse." This will make your case stronger. If the problem is getting severe, you'll provide people with new information and change the story of your case: The boat's not just taking on water—it's sinking.

If You Heard "We Can Approve Only Part of the Project"

What if your case has three parts but the decision makers only approve one? Or they sign off on the first phase of your project but ask you to come back in six months or more to request the additional funding? This happens more often than people think. It's frustrating, but it doesn't have to demotivate you and your team. Instead, focus on the fact that the committee liked your idea and want to move it forward.

Approval of just one part of your project is particularly common at companies that use a tollgate process. If this is the situation you're in, ask the review committee what risks or questions need to be resolved by the time you reach the first milestone. Then proceed as though your project will be fully funded. That will give you the best sense of whether the project will be a success. At the end of the funding period, be prepared to go back and explain which of your assumptions held true and which didn't. For instance, you might have determined that the product cost can be 10% less than planned or that the launch date will need to change by three months. Since you documented the source of all your original numbers and assumptions, it will be easy to check with those individuals for updates. Prepare to come back and present the business case again with updated information on the benefits or costs based on what you learned so far.

The most common scenario, however—and the most challenging—is when the decision makers come back and say, "OK, we know you wanted $2 million, but what can you do for $1 million?" When asked if you can do the project or reach the same goals with less time or money, never say yes right away. Instead, tell the reviewers that you'll get back to them—very quickly—so you have time to redo the business case with those new constraints.

When you commit to doing just part of the project, resist the temptation to overpromise. First, don't do an across-the-board cut. If the committee wants you to submit a proposal for a project that costs 30% less, don't try to do everything the original case did with 30% less resources. It's better to restructure the project completely. Ask yourself and your team: What is a viable business opportunity that we can fund with this much money to achieve a portion of the goal? Can we drop the European sales arm? Can we cut down the rollout time? Second, don't agree to a cut in resources without a cut in the benefits. This creates an almost impossible situation. If your original case promised $800,000 in revenue from the new product but now you're asked to cut the budget by 20%, chances are you won't be able to realize the full $800,000. You'll need to bring that number down as well. After all, if you don't have a full tank of gas, you can't go as far.

You'll be prepared for this conversation if you run several scenarios in your spreadsheet ahead of your presentation (as described in the *HBR Guide to Building Your Business Case*). It's great if you have those numbers in your back pocket, but if not, go back and rerun your numbers. Fortunately, this is pretty easy if you've structured your spreadsheet well. Simply create another tab and change the relevant figures.

It's rare that a company can afford to fund every good idea. Instead of harping on the cuts you needed to make, focus your team on creating and implementing a new plan that will help pave the way for the rest of your project to be approved later on.

If You Heard "Yes, Let's Move Ahead"

First, celebrate. Open a bottle of champagne or take your team out for dinner. Then get to work. After all, the decision makers just opened a door and you've got to walk through it. You'll need to figure out how you transition from getting your project approved to implementing it.

Don't wait for the check. In most companies, a formal funding mechanism doesn't exist—nobody actually writes you a check. More likely you're told: OK, you've got the resources and people you need; get started.

After your celebration, the first step is to set up your project management process. Some companies have a methodology for this. If that's the case at your organization, reach out to your contact in the project planning or management group. This person can set you up with the appropriate tools, templates, checklists, or software to start the project.

If there isn't a formal process at your company, get the project moving yourself. Start by gathering your team and working on a project charter. Review the high-level implementation plan you outlined in the case and make sure it's still actionable. And keep the business case handy. It was the initial road map for the project and it will be helpful to refer to as you structure the work. See the *HBR Guide to Project Management* for more information on tools and templates to help you manage a project effectively.

You've succeeded in getting the organization behind your solution to an important business need, but this is just the beginning. Think of it as building a house: You've chosen the architect and the builders, you've agreed on a blueprint, the bank has approved the funding, and you have a rough schedule and budget—but you haven't broken ground yet. Now comes the real work.

Raymond Sheen, PMP, is the president of Product & Process Innovation, a consulting firm specializing in project management, product development, and process improvement. He is the author, with Amy Gallo, of the *HBR Guide to Building Your Business Case* (Harvard Business Review Press, 2015). **Amy Gallo** is a contributing editor at *Harvard Business Review* and is the author of the *HBR Guide to Dealing with Conflict* (Harvard Business Review Press, 2017).

Evaluating and Prioritizing an Initiative Portfolio

CHAPTER 4

Which Initiatives Should You Implement?

by Sam Bodley-Scott and Alan P. Brache

Allocating financial and human resources to balance short-term and long-term needs is a perpetual challenge for organizations. Because of the complexity and risk around these decisions, the process for evaluating projects must be rigorous and rational. We recommend following a process we call *optimal project portfolio*, or **OPP**. Implementing OPP involves five steps:

1. **Develop project-prioritization criteria.** Are you more interested in achieving a short-term sales

---

Adapted from *Harvard Management Update*, September 2009 (product #U0904B).

boost or in furthering your three-year strategic plan? Increasing customer ratings or reducing costs? The criteria you use to prioritize projects will be determined by your main goals.

2. **Analyze resource capacity.** How much time do your people have to give to special projects? What's the availability of needed machinery or shared services?

3. **Gather and organize information on current and planned projects.** How many projects are currently underway or in the planning stage? How much time and money is each project currently consuming? How many projects are related to product development and how many are related to safety and security issues?

4. **Evaluate the project portfolio.** Are there any projects that can be combined? Which initiatives should get the green light, and which should be shelved for now? Which can run in tandem?

5. **Implement an ongoing project-portfolio-management process.** What steps can you take to make project review and prioritization an ongoing effort?

This methodology works at the division and unit levels as well; indeed, in large organizations, implementing the OPP process on several levels is advisable. In this chapter, we'll detail what goes into each step and show you what OPP looks like in action.

1. Develop Project-Prioritization Criteria

A project portfolio, like an investment portfolio, should be diversified. It typically contains a mix of strategic and tactical initiatives, growth-driven and cost-driven initiatives, and customer-focused and employee-focused projects. The criteria used to prioritize current and potential projects generally fall into these categories:

- Further the strategy.

- Balance the needs to weather the current economic storm and to prepare for the better days that lie ahead.

- Increase sales.

- Establish a competitive advantage, or eliminate a competitive disadvantage.

- Increase customer satisfaction.

- Reduce cost.

- Increase employee satisfaction and retention.

- Ensure regulatory compliance.

The following example shows how a U.S.-based multinational consumer products company determined what criteria it would use to prioritize projects.

During the process of formulating a new strategy, the organization's top management team concluded that its primary competitive advantages were the strength of its brand and its ability to facilitate customer-to-customer communication. As the team members brainstormed ways to leverage these strengths, they identified an opportunity to offer a smartphone-based digital platform. Because they were concerned that this opportunity would be stifled in their legacy environment, they set up a separate company to pursue it.

The executive team of the new company began with a list of 30 strategic initiatives. Using the company's new mandate as a basis, the group identified the following screening and priority-setting criteria:

- Maximize speed to market.

- Support the delivery of the strategic proposition.

- Support use of the parent brand.

- Maximize return on investment.

- Minimize business risk.

- Maximize value to external partners.

- Minimize time to recruit and deploy the right employees.

- Support robust process and IT development.

The team quickly realized that the criteria were not equally important, so they weighted each criterion on a 10-point scale and sought to strike a balance between

FIGURE 4-1

How one company assigned a priority score to initiatives

| | | | | | | | Potential initiatives | | | | | |
| Balance of criteria | | | | | Priority-setting criteria | | Set up Japanese business | | Develop marketing plan and planning process | | Build performance management process | |
Internal	External	Long-term	Short-term	Weighting			Score out of 10	Weighted score	Score out of 10	Weighted score	Score out of 10	Weighted score
	•		•	10	Maximize speed to market		7	70	5	50	3	30
•		•		10	Maximize return on investment		7	70	6	60	8	80
•	•	•		6	Support use of parent brand		8	48	4	24	0	0
•		•	•	4	Minimize business risk		2	8	8	32	5	20
	•	•		3	Maximize value to external partners		7	21	3	9	1	3

Prioritization score	Set up Japanese business	Develop marketing plan	Build performance management
	342	277	173

Resource requirements

	Set up Japanese business	Develop marketing plan	Build performance management
Marketing	•	•	
Process design	•	•	•
Finance	•	•	•
HR	•		•
	Go	Go	No go

short-term and long-term needs, and external and internal focus. (See the left-hand columns of figure 4-1.)

2. Analyze Resource Capacity

When it comes to committing to a certain number of initiatives, you don't want to bite off more than you can chew, but you also don't want to squander opportunities to, for example, improve systems, better serve customers, or boost employee development and retention. So you need to take the measure of your resource capacity—not only the number of available person-hours by organization unit but also the availability of machinery, facilities, and materials.

Those conscientious executives who are aware of their project capacity in good times have to update their numbers to reflect any reductions in available funds or people.

3. Gather and Organize Information on Current and Planned Projects

Next is to assess the likely impact of each current or planned initiative as well as what resources it will require. Collecting the information necessary to do this should be relatively straightforward if there is a project office or some other structure with a finger on the pulse of all initiative activity. If not, a bit of digging ("initiative forensics") is required. Analysts with a healthy appetite for detail and significant project management experience should interview executives, project managers, and others in a position to know what initiatives are afoot and record their findings.

Their tasks will include:

- Identifying the projects that are currently underway, those that have been approved but not yet launched, and those under consideration.

- Answering the following questions for each project:

  - What is the purpose of this project?

  - What would be the short- and long-term consequences of scaling back, delaying, or eliminating this project?

- What are its deliverables (outputs)?

- In what phase (definition, planning, or implementation) is it?

- Who are the people involved, and what are their roles?

- How much time and money is the project currently consuming?

- Sorting the projects by:

  - **Project type.** For example, projects related to product development, marketing, customer service, revenue, safety, and so on.

  - **Resource type.** Which people from each department or site, which machines, which facilities, and how much money are dedicated to project work?

  - **Time.** When are the projects scheduled to begin and end, and when will the resources be needed?

  - **Objective.** For example, does it contribute to short-term cost reductions, long-term revenue growth, preparedness for a recessionary environment, or entry into a new market?

4. Evaluate the Project Portfolio

Now the really hard work begins. Based on the wealth of information gathered, the executive team embarks on the wrenching but necessary process of deciding:

- Which projects should be combined.

- Which projects are "go" and which are "no go."

- Which "go" projects will be deferred until resources become available.

- The priority of the "go" projects.

- The sequence of the "go" projects; some projects may be able to run simultaneously, while some may need to follow others.

In this step, the project team for the organization in our example—the consumer products company spin-off formed to develop a digital-service offering—put the work it had done in step 1 on establishing and weighting project criteria to good use. First, the team members assessed how well each of the 30 potential projects they had identified met each criterion and assigned scores from 1 to 10 to the projects according to how well they measured up to the various criteria. Their approach ensured that those projects that best met all the criteria received the highest priority.

While no projects were eliminated during this process, the team was able to place each project into one of four priority categories:

- **Mission-critical.** Most deserving of precious resources at this time.

- **Important.** Will pursue now but with less emphasis than initiatives deemed mission-critical.

- **Wait-listed.** Will tackle as soon as resources are freed up from initiatives in categories 1 and 2.

- **On hold.** Will not undertake or plan for at
  this time.

This categorization guided both resource allocation and sequence.

Armed with priority and sequence, team members moved to establish the schedule. They used their capacity analysis—the output of steps 2 and 3—to determine how much of this work they could take on at any one time. For example, they determined that a project in the second category ("Important")—"Develop brand guidelines"—would exhaust their marketing resources. Other initiatives requiring marketing expertise would need to be scheduled after the brand work was completed. The full set of projects was scheduled over 16 months.

5. Implement an Ongoing Project-Portfolio-Management Process

Realizing that creating a project portfolio couldn't be a onetime effort, the digital spin-off's project team established a process for the ongoing review and update of its project portfolio and an infrastructure for supporting project excellence. In this final step of the OPP process, the team embedded rational initiative portfolio management into their nascent organization by:

- Adding a standing "initiative portfolio
  review" item to the agenda of monthly staff
  meetings.

- Scheduling a comprehensive half-day portfolio
  review meeting every six months.

WHY DO SO MANY INITIATIVES FAIL?

by Peter LaCasse and Travis Manzione

Most organizations, regardless of their size, industry, or degree of complexity, struggle with their strategic initiatives—with identifying, prioritizing, planning, and/or managing them. Although these organizations recognize the vital role initiatives play in advancing their strategic goals, most fail to ensure their initiatives are actually doing so. Each year, they spend millions on the wrong initiatives and waste millions more on unsuccessful ones.

Why do so few initiatives achieve the desired results? Among the key reasons we've found:

- *Initiative overload.* The organization tries to implement too many initiatives at once and ends up spreading its resources too thin.

- *Lack of alignment.* One or more initiatives may not be well aligned to the strategy.

- Designing and installing a process and template for new initiative proposals.

- Designating a person in the finance department as "mission control" for all initiatives consuming more than 200 person-hours and/or $50,000 in capital.

What's more, the project team committed to re-evaluating the portfolio once the economic tide started to turn.

- **Conflicting initiatives.** One initiative is at cross-purposes with another.

- **Inability to prioritize the initiative pool.** Leaders might not agree on which initiatives should be made top priority, resulting in the adoption of initiatives that are strategically less relevant and therefore garner only lukewarm support.

- **Insufficient resources.** The right resources are either not made available or not applied.

- **Poor project management.** Initiatives are either mismanaged or not managed through to completion.

Adapted from "Initiative Management: Putting Strategy into Action" by Peter LaCasse and Travis Manzione, *Balanced Scorecard Report*, November–December 2007 (product #B0711B).

Getting to Results

Setting priority on initiatives ensures that an organization—whether it be a multinational behemoth, a 25-employee startup, or a midsize division—is not launching more initiatives than it can accomplish successfully and that those launched are those likely to have the greatest impact. If an organization did nothing else to improve the quality of its projects, prioritizing them would add significant value. Determining where to focus finite resources is a critical step in enabling an organization to survive the downturn and emerge from it ready to leap ahead. (See the sidebar "Why Do So Many Initiatives Fail?")

Sam Bodley-Scott is head of strategy at DAL Food. He was formerly the global director of strategy at the international consulting firm Kepner-Tregoe. **Alan P. Brache** is cofounder of the Rummler-Brache Group. He was formerly technical director of the strategy group at Kepner-Tregoe.

CHAPTER 5

A Better Way to Set Strategic Priorities

by Derek Lidow

Smart leaders understand that their job requires them to identify trade-offs, choosing what *not* to do as much as what *to* do. Grading the importance of various initiatives in an environment of finite resources is a primary test of leadership.

To meet this challenge, leaders often turn to rank ordering their priorities; it is natural and easy to make a list. When I work with leaders on the crucial task of priority setting, however, I caution against rank ordering.

Adapted from content posted on hbr.org, February 13, 2017 (product #H03FAI).

It can be tremendously demotivating to managers to be assigned a rank, and it all but guarantees dissension and turf wars between team members.

A better way to establish priorities is to put rank ordering aside and return to first principles. There are three interdependent variables that are essential for executing any initiative: objectives, resources, and timing. You can't produce a project's desired effect without precise objectives, ample resources, and a reasonable time frame. If you push or pull on one leg of this triangle, you must adjust the others.

All three variables are important, but resources reign supreme. Resources are what enable an objective to be accomplished within a set time; without dedicated means, an initiative is pure fantasy. Once a leader decides what resources will be allocated to achieve which objectives over what periods of time, there is no more need for ranking. The leader will be forced to acknowledge three kinds of priorities: critical, important, and desirable.

Three Types of Strategic Priorities

A *critical* priority is an objective that must be successfully accomplished within a specified amount of time, no matter what. For example, it might be critical that a company win a new order (which will be awarded on a given date) from a major customer, or get a factory fully operational by a certain day. If the objective of winning the order is set and the timing is nonnegotiable, then the only element you can manipulate is resources (money, people, equipment). If the leader is sincere about the priority, then they must make all the resources requested available to the project manager. Though leaders may not realize it, declaring a project "critical" implies that it must be accompanied by a de facto blank check, enabling the manager to draw on all other available resources within the organization. And all critical priorities are, by definition, equal within the category.

An *important* priority, on the other hand, is an effort that can have a significant positive impact on performance. For these initiatives, resources are fixed and the variable is either time or the objective. For example, an organization may have an aspirational goal but fix the resources that it feels it can afford to invest over a specified time. A leader might say, "Let's assign Miguel and Aisha to this project full time for the next quarter." The organization, if it is operating rationally, should be willing to accept however much improvement it can get from that fixed investment. Alternatively, an organization may declare that it will invest a specified amount of resources for as long as it takes to achieve an objective: "We're going to assign Miguel and Aisha to install the new software, however long that will take." An important priority implies that the organization be understanding when the objective is variable and patient when time may vary.

A *desirable* priority is an effort in which resources and time are both variables. The organization desires an outcome but cannot absolutely commit specific resources over any specifiable time period: "Whenever Miguel and Aisha are not required on our critical product launch, they will work on installing the software upgrade." Progress will be made only when and if resources become available.

Because resources are fixed for all critical and important priorities, the potential "blank check" resources that may be required to hit a critical project must all come from desirable tasks. You cannot in good conscience set a critical priority unless you also designate desirable projects from which resources will be immediately transferred to the critical objective when required.

Allocate Resources and Plan Priorities

Once you have identified critical, important, and desirable projects, you can begin to identify appropriate objectives, resources, and time for each one. Use the following four-step process, which is also illustrated in figure 5-1.

Step 1. List in one column the resources (people, money, highly constrained elements like a sample bus for demonstrating products) available for all proposed projects. For example, you might have 10 salespeople on the East Coast, 7 on the West Coast, 4 in the Midwest, and 3 in the South; a travel budget of $10,000; and one sample bus.

Step 2. List across the top row the projects, improvements, or initiatives you want to accomplish with those resources with any existing time constraints. For example, you might write, "Renew clients in all four regions; win a contract with IBM by the time your new plant opens on March 1; get Salesforce.com in all regions but on a staggered schedule."

Step 3. Indicate in the appropriate cell how the available resources would be allocated in a scenario where everything proceeds as expected. For example, 3 salespeople in each region might be devoted to renewing customer contracts, while 12 salespeople, the sample bus, and half of the travel budget might go toward winning the IBM contract.

Step 4. Declare which one or two projects are critical, designating which additional resources from the matrix can be called on by the critical objectives when and if needed. (If you declare more than one project critical, you must keep in mind that they cannot potentially depend upon the same pool of on-call resources.) For example, if the IBM contract is critical, you would ask the project head—in this case, your lead IBM salesperson— what additional resources might conceivably be needed if the going gets tough, and where those resources might come from. That could include some of the IT resources from the Salesforce implementation on the East Coast, which means that the Salesforce effort is now categorized as desirable and that you cannot expect your people to fulfill the objective by a certain time. Projects that are not critical but aren't on call to potentially provide resources to a critical project now fall into the important category, where time or the objective is flexible.

As the projects and resources are listed and the group figures out how best to allocate resources and

FIGURE 5-1

Example spreadsheet for strategic priorities

Step 1: List resources

East Coast sales (10 people)						
West Coast sales (7 people)						
Midwest sales (4 people)						
Southern U.S. sales (3 people)						
Travel ($10,000)						
Sample bus						
IT resources (6 people)						

Step 2: Add projects, improvements, or initiatives

	Renew all clients	Win IBM contract by March 1	East Install Salesforce by March 1	West Install Salesforce by ?	Midwest Install Salesforce by ?	South Install Salesforce by ?
East Coast sales (10 people)						
West Coast sales (7 people)						
Midwest sales (4 people)						
Southern U.S. sales (3 people)						
Travel ($10,000)						
Sample bus						
IT resources (6 people)						

Step 3: Allocate resources

	Renew all clients	Win IBM contract by March 1	East Install Salesforce by March 1	West Install Salesforce by ?	Midwest Install Salesforce by ?	South Install Salesforce by ?
East Coast sales (10 people)	3 people	7 people				
West Coast sales (7 people)	3 people	4 people				
Midwest sales (4 people)	3 people	1 person				
Southern U.S. sales (3 people)	3 people					
Travel ($10,000)	$5,000	$5,000				
Sample bus		X				
IT resources (6 people)			6 people			

Step 4: Decide on one or two critical projects

	Renew all clients	Win IBM contract by March 1	East Install Salesforce ~~by March 1~~	West Install Salesforce by ?	Midwest Install Salesforce by ?	South Install Salesforce by ?
East Coast sales (10 people)	3 people	7 people				
West Coast sales (7 people)	3 people	4 people				
Midwest sales (4 people)	3 people	1 person				
Southern U.S. sales (3 people)	3 people					
Travel ($10,000)	$5,000	$5,000				
Sample bus		X				
IT resources (6 people)			6 people			

time constraints among the potential initiatives, this matrix becomes a strategy document. As projects are completed, leaders can revisit the process to reallocate resources that have been freed up. They can also reallocate resources if a crisis occurs—which by definition creates a critical priority. The same is true with a change of strategy.

The transparent allocation of resources and the specifying of responses to changed conditions align the team and head off dissension. Managers no longer feel that giving up resources reduces their status. They are playing an essential role in executing a critical priority. And they are content to be governed by the fair, inexorable logic of realistic priority setting instead of rank ordering that doesn't add up.

Derek Lidow teaches entrepreneurship, innovation, and creativity at Princeton. He was the founder and former CEO of iSuppli Corporation and is the author of *Startup Leadership*. His newest book is *Building on Bedrock*. Follow him on Twitter @DerekLidow.

CHAPTER 6

Too Many Projects

by Rose Hollister and Michael D. Watkins

If "the essence of strategy is choosing what not to do," as Michael Porter famously said in a seminal HBR article, then the essence of execution is truly not doing it. That sounds simple, but it's surprisingly hard for organizations to kill existing initiatives, even when they don't align with new strategies. Instead, leaders keep layering on initiatives, which can lead to severe overload at levels below the executive team.

Sometimes leaders are unaware of all the initiatives underway and their impact on the organization. In other cases organizational politics conspires to let initiatives continue long after they should have run their course. Either way, overload can result in costly productivity and quality problems and employee burnout. With record

---

Reprinted from *Harvard Business Review*, September–October 2018 (product #R1805C).

low unemployment, companies that do not adjust the workload are also at risk of losing valuable talent. One leader who used to head up talent consulting at a human capital firm told us in an interview, "While I enjoyed and respected my team and found the work motivating, the pace was unsustainable. I chose to leave before I had a heart attack."

In many organizations, the alarm bells for initiative overload ring when engagement survey results drop or turnover levels rise—or both. At one *Fortune* 500 retail company, for example, internal studies showed that store managers had more duties than they could accomplish in a standard workweek. Instead of moderating the demands of the job, their bosses expected them to prioritize and juggle. Yet with business results faltering and customer service scores declining, the senior executive team realized that a new approach was needed and recommended that a task force of high-potential leaders assess the impact of initiatives on frontline store managers.

The task force found that many departments were simultaneously launching initiatives that required store managers' attention, in areas such as product launches, training, customer service, and IT. A comprehensive review revealed that more than 90 distinct initiatives had gotten underway in the previous six months. Store managers were expected to absorb and act on them while dealing with high customer volume and managing the staff. All these demands took their toll. Some outlets failed to meet company expectations and forecasts, and adoption rates for new initiatives dropped, because the organization just couldn't process them all.

When company leaders received the report, they realized that they had to be more disciplined about setting limits and priorities, rather than expect store managers to keep shouldering everything. The country president assigned a senior leader to act as the gatekeeper between functional departments and store managers. Departments could no longer reach out directly to managers with new work expectations—those were funneled through the leader, who assessed priorities and protected the managers from impossible work demands. This change allowed store managers to focus; doing less yielded better results on the key initiatives and priorities.

In our consulting work with dozens of businesses, we've seen the consequences of overload play out again and again across a range of industries. In conversations and interviews in a wide variety of organizations, capacity is a frequent topic: Leaders feel pressured to do more with fewer resources. We've identified several root causes, which we'll discuss here so that you can spot the risks in your company. Organizations tend to rely on flawed fixes, so we'll also explain why those typically fail and what works better.

The Roots of the Problem

Why does initiative overload happen? We have observed seven causes:

Impact blindness

As the *Fortune* 500 retailer learned, executive teams can be oblivious to the number and cumulative impact of the initiatives they have in progress. Many organizations lack mechanisms to identify, measure, and manage the demands that initiatives place on the managers and employees who are expected to do the work. In practice, it can be challenging to measure the load across an organization, because of initiative volume, company complexity and size, and insufficient tracking tools. But as the example above shows, it can be done if the business dedicates resources to making it happen.

Multiplier effects

Most senior leaders have a line of sight into their own groups' initiatives and priorities but a limited view of other groups' activities. Because functions and units often set their priorities and launch initiatives in isolation, they may not understand the impact on neighboring functions and units. Suppose, for example, that an organization consists of five units. If each one undertakes three initiatives, each of which requires some resources from two other units, then frontline managers in each unit are effectively juggling nine initiatives. And this assumes an even distribution of impact; if some units have particularly critical or scarce resources, their load could be far greater.

Political logrolling

Executives tend to be strongly invested in some "signature" projects and may garner resources for them through implicit agreements with their peers: "I will support your initiatives if you support mine." In the world of legislative politics, this is known as logrolling, a term reportedly coined in 1835 by U.S. Congressman

Davy Crockett as a metaphor derived from the old cus-tom of neighbors' assisting one another with the moving of logs. In organizations it leads to a pileup of promises to fulfill—and projects that just won't die. This can hap-pen even after funding has been officially cut, because leaders may have their own deep pockets of funding and the decision-making power to keep their initiatives mov-ing forward.

Unfunded mandates

In the world of politics this term is used when legisla-tures pass laws that require certain things to happen but don't provide funding for implementation. Similarly, in business, executive teams often task their organizations with meeting important goals without giving manag-ers and their teams the necessary resources to accom-plish them. In one major acquisition in which we were involved, the executive team spent tens of millions of dollars on consulting to design the new, combined or-ganization's strategy, structure, systems, and staffing but provided no funding to support the critical work of transition and integration. Largely as a result of conflicts between "us" and "them," the acquiring company lost most of the acquired entity's best talent—the retention of which had been a core goal. This is not an isolated ex-ample: Initiatives are often launched without having re-sources dedicated to them.

Band-Aid initiatives

When projects are launched to provide limited fixes to significant problems, the result can be a proliferation of initiatives, none of which may adequately deal with root causes. We have seen companies make substantial investments in training programs in response to superficial assessments of the skills required, or provide limited support for integrating the new skills into day-to-day practice.

Cost myopia

Another partial fix that can exacerbate overload is cutting people without cutting the related work. This happens when organizations fixate on lowering head count (an obvious way to rein in human capital costs) but overlook the price they might pay—in employee burnout, performance strain, and turnover—for expecting the remaining people to take on the tasks of those who have left. A leader at a consumer products firm described the problem in an interview: "We had planned to reengineer our processes, but it did not happen. The impact is that our people are working harder with fewer resources."

Initiative inertia

Finally, companies often lack the means (and the will) to stop existing initiatives. Sometimes that's because they have no "sunset" process for determining when to close things down. A project might have been vital for the business when it launched, but later the rationale no longer exists—and yet the funding and the work continue. For example, for decades many organizations used so-called mystery shoppers to gather customer feedback and evaluate customer service. With the internet, companies can now gather feedback and data directly from their customers. But many have been slow to make the shift, because parting with a well-oiled machine—even one that is clearly dated—means switching to less-tested systems that require all-new competencies. The habits and the infrastructure for mystery shoppers are already built. Capturing, understanding, and valuing customer data gathered online requires time and different skill sets. So, many traditional companies follow the lead of upstarts, which do not have to unlearn old, comfortable approaches: They hire new leaders with the right skills to help make the transition.

What Doesn't Work

Recognizing initiative overload is an important first step—but leaders must then take meaningful action. Too often, though, they resort to strategies that either have no impact or make the problem worse. For instance:

Prioritizing by function or department

Leaders are most comfortable setting priorities within their own area, because they know that territory best, but this does not allow them to recognize the cumulative impact of initiatives across groups. For example, a top goal for finance might be to adopt a new expense program across the enterprise. Even if it's the right decision for the company, learning the new system by trial and error or through training places extra demands on leaders outside the finance function. Designated "superusers" put in even more time than most, coaching their colleagues on day-to-day use and fielding questions as they arise, and that eats into the time they can spend on their

DOES YOUR ORGANIZATION HAVE A PROBLEM?

The first step in dealing with initiative overload is to honestly assess and acknowledge the problem. Ask yourself the questions below to gauge whether your organization is at risk. Then total up the yeses—those are red flags. If you have *more than four*, you may need to better manage the number or timing of initiatives.

Do leaders often talk about the need to cut back on the number of new initiatives? **Yes/No**

Does a significant amount of work and team time revolve around launching and supporting initiatives? **Yes/No**

Does the organization lack a central group that reviews all current initiatives? **Yes/No**

Does the organization lack processes for quantifying impact and prioritizing initiatives? **Yes/No**

Are multiple initiatives being launched simultaneously? **Yes/No**

Are initiatives often launched without coordination across units and functions? **Yes/No**

Are initiatives launched without business cases? **Yes/No**

Are initiatives launched without success metrics? **Yes/No**

Does the current number of initiatives have a negative impact on productivity and prioritization? **Yes/No**

Are initiatives often started mid-cycle in response to new external or internal demands? **Yes/No**

Is stopping or slowing down initiatives countercultural? **Yes/No**

Are legacy projects renewed without a regular assessment of current need or effectiveness? **Yes/No**

Are initiatives launched even when resources are already stretched? **Yes/No**

Are people expected to absorb new demands without stopping past projects? **Yes/No**

Are projects launched without a full analysis of ongoing support needs? **Yes/No**

Are initiatives launched without a "sunset," or stopping, process having been identified? **Yes/No**

Is the success of an initiative evaluated primarily by the leaders who launched and own the project? **Yes/No** own teams' projects. Of course, all those demands butt up against recurring processes that consume everyone's time across the organization: Managers must create and manage budgets for finance, document individual and team performance for HR, undergo ethics or sexual harassment training for legal, and so on.

So priorities can't be set in a vacuum. Senior leaders need to encourage transparent conversations across functions about work volume, initiative demands, and resources—this top-down message is critical. But they must also be receptive to constructive feedback from bottom-up conversations, and too often they just don't want to hear about what people *can't* do. In such an atmosphere, employees are afraid to voice concerns about workload or to admit having limits, because of the risk to their careers, so they keep mum. And without that input, leaders lack a full view of demands across the enterprise and can't prioritize accordingly.

Establishing overall priorities without deciding what to cut

Leadership teams often engage in prioritization exercises that define and communicate where people should focus their energy. However, they undermine those efforts if they don't also do the hard work of explicitly deciding what trade-offs to make and what has to stop. At a real estate company we worked with, the leadership team decided to simultaneously launch more than a dozen initiatives. Project teams were formed and expected to produce results quickly. The desired outcomes were achieved, but at a steep cost: Key contributors decided to exit the organization rather than meet the escalated demands—exceedingly long hours and overwhelming new responsibilities.

Making across-the-board initiative cuts

When leaders ask all departments or functions to cut their budgets or initiatives by a given amount—say, 10% to 20%—each group finds its own way to comply. However, this approach to reduction doesn't take into consideration overall organizational priorities and interdependencies. As a result, cuts to projects in one function, such as IT or marketing, can undermine the ability of other functions to deliver critical projects. For example, as part of overall cost containment, the IT department at a hospitality company had to cut costs by 20%. So it moved to a model based on self-service and outsourcing and eliminated on-site, in-person computer support. Although IT achieved its cuts, all the other functions spent more time resolving their IT issues.

What Does Work

While challenging, it is possible to fight initiative overload and concentrate organizational resources on strategically essential projects. For example, CBIZ, a growing business-services company, has become much stricter about deciding which projects can move forward. Marina Davis, the company's director of organization and talent development, told us in an interview, "We look at each initiative through two lenses: One, does it have a positive impact on the business? And two, does it have a positive impact on the culture? As we continue to gain speed, we are being very careful about choosing what we will and will not take on at this time."

Similarly, senior leaders at the real estate firm mentioned earlier—the one that launched so many initiatives at once—began to see a need for change. Although they had pushed for business transformation that year, they didn't want that pace to become the new normal. So they watched for signs of that in the next year and were surprised at the sheer volume of budget dollars being requested for even *more* initiatives, most of them internal—all-staff meetings, leadership development events, planning meetings, IT launches, and HR training. Although the company financials were strong enough to support the requests, the firm needed to focus more intently on hands-on sales, and the executive team worried that the other proposed initiatives could get in the way. To assess that concern, they asked functional leaders to break down travel budgets and time spent in and out of the office, along with development funding and facility and food costs, for each requested initiative. The human capital implications then became clear: Together, the internal meetings and events would demand more than 30% of managers' time. After discussing the matter with the senior team and targeting a lower percentage of time away from customers, the CEO and the CFO decided which initiatives to keep and which to cut, favoring those that were important to generating business. The following year managers spent more time in the field and less in training and planning sessions, and the demands on their time became more manageable.

As these examples show, fighting initiative overload requires the will and the discipline to make and enforce hard choices. Here's a step-by-step process that can guide you.

1. Get a true count of current initiatives across the enterprise, to see if your organization is suffering from overload. (See the sidebar "Does Your Organization Have a Problem?")

2. Assess all the initiatives currently underway. For each one, identify the business need, the required budget, the head count allocation, and the business impact.

3. Have senior leaders work together to establish priorities in an integrated way. The discussion must be driven by the top leadership team and informed by candid feedback from below to ensure sufficient decreases in initiatives.

4. Put in place a sunset clause for each initiative, identifying an end date for funding and a head count allocation, so that projects do not consume resources year after year unless they are making a significant business impact.

5. In subsequent yearly planning, require each initiative to reapply for funding and other resources. Mandated business cases should demonstrate the value to the organization.

6. Strongly communicate to the rest of the organization that stopping an initiative doesn't mean that it was a failure or lacked merit. Emphasize that there's simply a limit to how many great ideas the company can launch.

QUESTIONS TO ASK BEFORE YOU LAUNCH AN INITIATIVE

Analyzing the Project

- What problem is this initiative meant to fix?

- What data or other evidence tells us that this initiative will have the desired impact?

Assessing Resources

- What is the true human capital demand?

  - What resources (time, budget, and head count) are needed to design and launch the initiative?

  - In addition to the department that owns the initiative, what departments or functions will be tasked with supporting it?

  - What time commitments will be asked of leaders and staff members to attend meetings or develop the skills needed to understand or implement the initiative?

  - What resources will be needed to sustain it?

Of course, the best way to avoid initiative overload is to not allow it in the first place. That means building in rigorous reviews to impose discipline on when and how the organization launches initiatives—and keeping close tabs on whose time they consume, and how much. (See

- How does the human capital demand compare with the potential business impact? Does the cost outweigh the benefit?

- How will the organization determine whether it has the capacity to take on the initiative?

Sizing Up Stakeholder Support

- Who are the key stakeholders?

- What actions will be required to support the initiative?

- How fully is that support in place?

Setting Limits

- What trade-offs are we willing to make? In other words, if we do this, what *won't* get done?

- What's the sunset schedule and process?

the sidebar "Questions to Ask Before You Launch an Initiative.")

For companies already experiencing initiative overload, focusing on the benefits of cutting back can make the path forward somewhat easier. Organizations are at a great advantage when they learn how to say no, as Steve Jobs once put it, to the "hundred other good ideas that there are." They can then use their creative and productive energy more wisely, foster greater employee commitment and loyalty, and accomplish more in the areas that really matter.

———————

Rose Hollister is a leadership consultant at Genesis. She teaches courses on global leadership and change at Northwestern University, and she led the Leadership Institute at McDonald's from 2010 to 2017. **Michael D. Watkins** is a cofounder of Genesis, a professor at IMD Business School, and the author of *The First 90 Days* and *Master Your Next Move* (Harvard Business Review Press, 2013 and 2019 respectively).

CHAPTER 7

The Initiative Portfolio Review Process

by Keith Katz and Travis Manzione

While we've seen widespread improvement in prioritizing and selecting initiatives, organizations still have a long way to go in reporting on and managing them. This ongoing step is critical not only for assessing the progress of each initiative, but also for demonstrating the return each initiative is yielding (ROI, or return on initiative). It ensures the initiative's ongoing value to a company's overall initiatives, providing a dynamic cost/

Adapted from "Maximize Your 'Return on Initiatives' with the Initiative Portfolio Review Process," *Balanced Scorecard Report*, May–June 2008 (product #B0805C).

benefit assessment that tracks each initiative's impact on funding and resources.

All too often, initiatives continue to receive funding, even without a clearly identified "owner," the person who is accountable for performance. (In this article, "funding" initiatives refers not only to supporting their tangible, direct costs, but also to providing the full-time employees they require.)

Sometimes initiatives extend long beyond their proposed life, incurring cost overruns and failing to provide their intended benefit. Unanticipated obstacles and barriers can push an initiative off track. A change in organizational strategy can render a once-worthy initiative strategically irrelevant. In every case, the lack of sufficient information and oversight prevents leaders from making informed investment decisions.

A company's resources are, of course, finite, and it cannot fund all strategically relevant initiatives. It must make hard choices to prioritize those that promise the most strategic payoff. Each resource decision affects not only the funded initiative, but also all the proposed initiatives vying for limited resources. In other words, every investment carries an associated opportunity cost, as it displaces resources that might otherwise be available for other initiatives. For that reason, an organization should monitor initiatives to maximize their individual and collective impact on performance—and monitor them regularly.

A regular, formal review process helps companies track costs and benefits, obstacles, and strategic shifts that can radically alter an initiative's value and progress.

But it does more: It enables them to capture important opportunities as they arise. Good ideas do not emerge just once a year during the strategic planning process. When organizations relegate initiative review to a once-a-year strategic planning period, they lose the ability to dynamically allocate resources to capture new, emerging opportunities—or to replace underperforming initiatives with more promising ones, or even simply to adjust to existing initiatives' actual performance. So it's not enough to institute a formal annual review; companies should schedule regular reviews, at least two a year.

Take a Portfolio View

Initiatives have stand-alone value—their inherent value—as well as their value as a component of a larger portfolio supporting a strategic theme. Managing initiatives within portfolios provides accretive value; it recognizes that the sum of a cluster of initiatives is more than the sum of individual initiatives. Initiative portfolio management consists of four steps. In the first step, information collection, the company gathers essential information about an initiative's performance, including progress against milestones, variance from anticipated budget, and projected deviations from the ROI. It enters this information into a standardized reporting template that includes a high-level, qualitative analysis of performance and recommendations. The information on each initiative is consolidated into a master report, which, along with a summary review, creates an initiative portfolio analysis. This document (step two) primarily supports the initiative portfolio review (step three). In step four, leaders communicate their decisions about ongoing, as well as funded but not yet launched, initiatives to all affected parties. These include initiative sponsors and project teams, as well as those who would use the initiative's deliverables—for example, customer service reps awaiting new CRM software implementation.

The Initiative Portfolio Analysis Document

The initiative portfolio analysis (IPA) reports on status and becomes the basis for the initiative performance review (IPR). It is created and revised regularly, according to the review meeting schedule. (See figure 7-1.) The document is divided into two sections, a summary and a detail section. The summary organizes initiatives by theme, in this example, "Realize Operational Efficiencies." Alongside each initiative, we see its progress (% completion) and whether it is being managed cost effectively (budget, variance from budget) and generating the expected return (expected and actual financial impact)—the latter two being critical risk factors for initiative success. Some reports include a column for "lifetime return." "Financial impact" covers the period of initiative implementation. Some initiatives, like Project Zebra, generate benefits even before they are completed. Also included is an overall status indicator (green, yellow, or red); it is based on timing vs. plan, budget vs. plan, and benefits realized vs. plan.

The goal of Project Zebra is to reduce shrink—the amount of a retailer's net margin that is eroded by waste, theft, and product spoilage. This initiative was

FIGURE 7-1

Initiative performance analysis (IPA) document—Summary

This summary is for our hypothetical company's strategic theme "Realize Operational Efficiencies." Among other things, summaries illustrate that different initiatives return at different rates and time periods.

Theme: Realize operational efficiencies

Initiative name	Status	Percent completed	Budget	Variance from budget	Financial impact (expected)	Financial impact (realized)	Owner
Project Zebra	G	100%	$300K	$0K	$1,000K	$1,050K	Jennifer Smith
Project Lion	Y	90%	$250K	$20K	$365K	$365K	John Opal
Project Penguin	R	20%	$800K	$200K	$2,400K	$2,400K	Mike Faith

2020 Business impact (budgeted)			$1,350K	$0K	$3,765K		Executive team
2020 Business impact (actual)			$1,350K	$220K		$3,815K	Executive team

expected to reduce shrink by 3%, ultimately contributing to a $3 million cost savings. At an estimated cost of $300,000, it would take three months to implement and generate $1 million of immediate cost relief. The detail view (figure 7-2) assesses Project Zebra just after completion. It came in on budget and delivered an immediate benefit of $1.05 million—$50,000 more than projected.

Each initiative within the theme portfolio has its own detail page in the IPA, which includes all of the summary-level information for that initiative, along with qualitative analysis, recommendations, and milestone progress. In the analysis section, the owner of the initiative explains whether the initiative is performing as expected, addressing time, budget, and return parameters. If the initiative is off track, the owner offers recommendations or else proposes terminating the initiative altogether, if it appears unsalvageable. In the milestones section, the owner tracks progress by phase; for example, Project Zebra's first milestone was to "assess current inventory tracking system."

The Initiative Performance Review

In a strategy review meeting, objectives are the primary focus; generally, managers only discuss initiatives in the context of how they support an objective. In the IPR, initiatives are the sole topic, discussed in the context of their organizational benefits. At this half-day working session, managers review each initiative portfolio in detail, deciding what to do with poorly performing initiatives and evaluating proposed initiatives. The fundamental

FIGURE 7-2

IPA—Detail for Project Zebra

The detail report provides further data on each individual initiative, including qualitative analysis of results and benefits realized. For example, it would explain that new inventory tracking systems reduced theft by 90% and spoilage by 35%. This detail was the last one written for Project Zebra, at its successful completion.

Project Zebra	Initiative owner
May 31, 2020	Jennifer Smith

Objectives impacted
- Internal process objective
- Internal process objective

Description
The purpose of this initiative is to improve our operational efficiency. Reducing shrink by 3% will lead to an additional $3m in savings for the business.

Budget	$300K		Financial impact (budgeted)	$1,000K
Variance from budget	$0K		Financial impact (realized)	$1,050K
Start date	January 21, 2020		Percent complete	100%
End date	April 23, 2020			

Performance analysis

Recommendations

Status	Milestone/task	% Complete	Start	End	Responsible

purpose of the IPR is to maintain an optimal total initiative portfolio, allocating resources accordingly. Usually, only executive team members attend, but if a significant issue about a given initiative arises, the initiative sponsor might also participate.

The leaders discuss each initiative in detail. If necessary, they reallocate resources. They then turn to proposed initiatives. If a proposed initiative appears likely to generate greater return than an existing initiative that is underperforming, they decide to terminate it and launch the new project.

The IPR also provides an opportunity to discuss changes in organizational strategy that might affect any initiatives and dynamically reallocate budgeting toward projects that support the new strategy. Similarly, if the overall budget for an initiative portfolio changes, the IPR is the venue for reallocating funding to those initiatives that are generating the greatest results per invested dollar.

Finally, because the context of this meeting is analytical, it is largely free of the "pet project" or "pride of ownership" issues that can plague a strategy review meeting. The numbers are the focus of the meeting, and participants understand the purpose is to cut deadweight initiatives and substitute alternate projects when appropriate.

Frequency and Scheduling

How often and when to schedule a review are critical to ensuring IPR success. There must be enough time between meetings to allow managers to make an informed decision about the course of action for any underperforming initiatives, as well as sufficient time to take corrective action. If too much time elapses, however, an organization might lose opportunities to shift resources to initiatives with potentially greater impact. Best-practice companies find that quarterly IPR meetings are optimal; two more formal meetings allow for readjustments (for example, adding or canceling initiatives).

When should meetings occur? If a company follows a traditional budgeting cycle, the date for budget approval becomes the anchor for the IPR calendar. Organizations that have adopted rolling forecasts use major milestones—such as the dates they file financial reports to the market or board members—to establish an optimal schedule.

Roles

Establishing clear roles and responsibilities is critical to conducting reviews that lead to effective decision making about limited resources. Executive team members serve as the ultimate governing body, making final decisions based on the facts. Theme owners, some of whom are also executive team members, lead discussions about the performance of their initiative portfolio, and suggest ways to optimize the portfolio. They generally prepare for meetings with initiative sponsors, who oversee the day-to-day execution of individual initiatives. Since they coordinate with milestone owners and provide critical input on initiative performance, sponsors often play a vital role in developing reports.

The advantages of the initiative reporting and management process are similar to those of the rolling forecast. Rather than wait for a once-per-year budgetary cycle to propose and allocate discretionary funding, companies have the information to continually adjust their focus and resources to maximize the impact of each discretionary dollar invested.

———————

Keith Katz is Director of PwC Labs Innovation and Tech Strategy. He was formerly a consultant at the Palladium Group. **Travis Manzione** is an accomplished strategy and operations executive. He is Director of QHP Strategy at Boston Medical Center HealthNet Plan.

CHAPTER 8

Rebalance Your Initiative Portfolio

by Peter LaCasse

The concept of initiative portfolio management is derived from sound investment practice. A good financial adviser ensures that each client has a balanced portfolio, with an appropriate mix of investments in stocks, bonds, money market, and other asset classes. In choosing this mix, the adviser considers many factors, such as the client's date of retirement, future income needs, and risk tolerance, among others. As things change, the adviser tweaks the mix on an ongoing basis. For example, if stocks represent 40% of a client's portfolio but quarterly

---

Adapted from "Rebalance Your Initiative Portfolio to Manage Risk and Maximize Performance," *Balanced Scorecard Report*, September–October 2008 (product #B0809D).

returns from them exceed that percentage, the adviser will need to rebalance the stock allocation to maintain the portfolio's original risk levels.

Initiative portfolio management should follow this portfolio balancing approach, where you evaluate each project in the context of the total portfolio. Unfortunately, most companies select initiatives independently of one another, with little regard for their impact on

A CASE EXAMPLE

The web division of a large retail bank defined its five-year strategy in terms of four strategic themes: market share growth/business development (sales), market protection/maintaining customers (web channel use), process efficiency, and organizational learning. Division leaders wanted to focus on expanding the web as a sales channel without losing ground in the other areas. After developing strategic objectives and aligning existing projects with the themes, the leaders learned that the company was spending most of its discretionary dollars on retaining customers and driving web channel use—to the detriment of the other themes.

However, as the leaders pushed for more projects geared toward sales growth, they did not overlook the other elements of a balanced portfolio. To balance the portfolio's risk profile, they maintained a healthy investment in keeping their current customer base if the new product ideas failed to catch hold in the marketplace. They also made sure that the returns from their other efforts. They should review the business case for each initiative in the larger context to consider its impact on other initiatives. This prevents overweighting investments to short-term results that risk mortgaging the organization's future, prevents investing too much in a particular strategic theme at the expense of others, and simply helps avoid projects that are too risky. (See the sidebar "A Case Example.")

projects aligned to their short-, medium-, and long-term (division) targets. In the short run, they felt that by freeing up 20% of their discretionary spending and an even greater percentage of their employees' time, they could apply those resources to projects more closely aligned to the strategy. For example, they invested in building the capability to sell products that the company had never before sold on the internet, rather than in enhancements to online checking and savings account services.

Once an enterprise establishes portfolio categories based on its strategic themes, each business unit should use the portfolios to organize its discretionary spending. Units then present their project portfolios to enterprise leaders, who can more readily assess how well the portfolios are balanced against overall strategy. In reviewing the portfolios collectively, the leaders can ensure that each division is doing its part to support the strategy of the whole company.

Preparing Initiatives for a Portfolio Management Approach

Organizations that follow the disciplined initiative management process already have detailed information on each project. They have already developed a business case when first proposing an initiative. Initially a set of high-level assumptions within a concept document, the case is refined into a detailed proposal document once the idea is approved and/or sponsored. This document addresses the project's goals, strategic impact, financial costs and benefits, time to implement, time to benefit, skills and capabilities required, and implementation and impact risks. If the detailed proposal passes leadership review, companies finalize the business case and develop a project plan.

The detailed business case information enables companies to regularly evaluate their initiative portfolios. Canadian Blood Services (CBS), the nonprofit that manages Canada's blood supply provides a good example of this process. The organization's leadership team spent three days evaluating its initiative portfolios. The portfolios were based on CBS's strategic themes, "Safety," "Operational Excellence," and "Prepare for Tomorrow." The team seemed to have allocated its initiatives appropriately across the three themes. But when team members looked at risk and benefit levels within each theme, the portfolios now seemed off balance. For example, in the theme Prepare for Tomorrow (about expanding business into new areas), most of the initiatives were medium to low risk and of medium benefit. The only initiative actually designed to help CBS expand into new areas was focused on developing its (umbilical) cord blood bank capabilities. Team members recognized that the strategic theme focused on changing their business should contain initiatives that would truly transform it. This realization spurred conversation, leading to the idea of expanding into such areas as organ transplants and tissue bank services that could further capitalize on CBS's process expertise. Now the team could easily see the gaps in each portfolio and develop initiative ideas to fill them. According to CEO Graham Sher, this portfolio framework "allowed us to have the difficult conversations about which initiatives to include or eliminate," adding that the total cost of slashed initiatives "equaled millions of dollars." Balancing the initiative portfolio, Sher observes, has helped CBS make the link between strategy and operations explicit.

Portfolio analysis should be the first step in rebalancing the initiative portfolio, as it provides the necessary data for discussion and decision making. Leaders examine the amount invested (both financial and human resources) in each theme, the skills and capabilities required to deliver on the portfolio's initiatives, the organizational change required, the aggregate risk within the portfolio, and the anticipated changes and benefits. They then weigh these requirements against the organization's available budget and human resources, inventory of skills, and capacity to support change, as well as the desired level of performance. Portfolio analysis is often best represented in multiple formats, including graphical and written. (See the sidebar "Keeping It Honest.")

KEEPING IT HONEST

Many organizations struggle to justify their initiatives. Overzealous managers write business case proposals that claim unrealistic benefits or underestimate costs. But there is a way to ensure business case legitimacy and prevent ill-founded initiatives from passing muster. By making leaders accountable for each business case and incorporating initiative and portfolio performance into their regular strategy performance reviews, organizations can remove the bias and fluff from proposals. Knowing that they will be held accountable for delivering their forecasted benefits and working within their own estimated budgets, leadership team members tend to be more realistic. Embedding such accountability into the process will invariably result in more pleasant surprises than unfortunate miscalculations.

Figure 8-1 is an example of a nine-cell grid, a graphical tool for evaluating theme initiative portfolios. Initiatives are classified by their purpose ("stay in the race," "win the race," or "change the rules"), risk level, and time to benefit. This example represents an office-product company's portfolio of initiatives within its strategic theme of innovation. Projects 1, 3, and 4 involve enhancements to the company's stapler, pen, and desk organizer product lines. These projects, aimed at maintaining competitiveness,

FIGURE 8-1

The nine-cell grid for evaluating theme portfolios

This grid, an aid in portfolio analysis, provides a snapshot view of an office products company's initiative portfolio for its innovation theme. The five projects represented here run the gamut in terms of purpose (design improvements to transformational change), risk, and time-to-benefit.

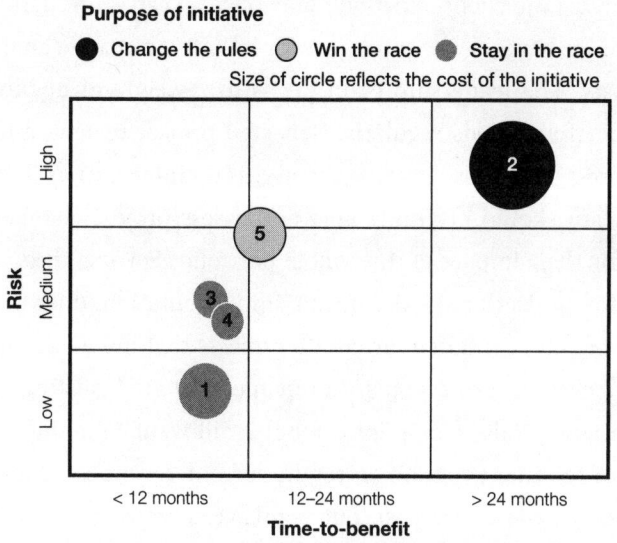

are relatively low cost and designed to yield short-term results. Project 2, a transformative initiative, involves developing an entirely new line of products, which will require creating new production capabilities, distribution partnerships, and new marketing. Project 5, geared toward gaining market share, involves marketing an existing product in a new region, which will require establishing a new distribution channel as well as a marketing campaign. The overall portfolio balances the short-term need to fend off competition and expand market share with the longer-term goal of exploring new markets and establishing new sources of revenue.

Making It Stick

Most investors would agree: A financial adviser who analyzes the client's portfolio only once a year is not doing his or her job. The same goes for initiative portfolio analysis. The leadership team needs to review and update portfolio needs regularly. Repeated project reviews and progress reports provide the necessary information. The team should promptly note and assess project changes for their impact on the whole portfolio. For instance, if one project's risks rise during implementation, does the portfolio contain appropriate projects that are a backup in case the project fails? Companies that are investing in a new product area, for example, will want to maintain an existing program to retain current revenues. Quarterly reviews are best, but regularity is most crucial; if left only to when executives have time, the reviews will almost never happen.

In practice, developing a portfolio review process takes time and effort. At first, initiative portfolio reviews often seem like regular project reviews, where leadership team members know little about parts of the business outside their direct functional responsibility. Over time, however, leaders realize the importance of understanding the entire business in making portfolio trade-off and balancing decisions. Discussions become more substantive, and leaders take a true team approach to making project portfolio decisions.

———————

Peter LaCasse is Chief Product Officer at Carnegie Learning. He was formerly Initiative Management Practice Leader at the Palladium Group.

Launching and Implementing Initiatives

CHAPTER 9

New Project? Don't Analyze—Act

by Leonard A. Schlesinger, Charles F. Kiefer, and Paul B. Brown

We all know how new projects happen in a predictable world: A team is assembled, a market analyzed, a forecast created, and a business plan written. Resources are then gathered, and the plan is set in motion.

But how do you launch new projects in an unpredictable environment? What's the best way to do it in an age when the proliferation of data and opinion makes truly decisive analysis impossible; when faraway events have immediate, unexpected impact; and when economic malaise has made companies reluctant to take big bets on unproven ideas?

Adapted from an article in *Harvard Business Review*, March 2012 (product #R1203R).

Take a page from the playbook of those who are experts in navigating extreme uncertainty while minimizing risk: serial entrepreneurs.

We and others in the academic and consulting communities have spent years studying these leaders and the logic they use to create new products, services, and business models in situations where the old methods of analyzing, forecasting, modeling, planning, and allocating don't work.

Some of the most surprising research comes from Saras D. Sarasvathy, an associate professor of business administration at the University of Virginia's Darden School of Business, whose in-depth study of 27 serial entrepreneurs revealed a number of common behaviors. Instead of starting with a predetermined goal, these entrepreneurs allow opportunities to emerge; instead of focusing on optimal returns, they spend more time considering their acceptable loss; and instead of searching for perfect solutions, they look for good-enough ones.

The point is that successful entrepreneurs don't just "think different." They translate that thinking into immediate action, often eschewing or ignoring analysis. Rather than predict the future, they try to create it. We have seen this firsthand in clients and former students who have launched businesses in a variety of industries. And look at Starbucks CEO Howard Schultz: Coffee sales had been steadily declining for two decades before he came up with the café concept that would grow into a multibillion-dollar business.

This logic shouldn't be limited to entrepreneurs working outside the bounds of traditional organizations. (After all, Schultz first tested his café idea when Starbucks was a small retailer of coffee beans, teas, and spices, and he was its director of marketing.) We believe that any manager can—and should—follow the same process when confronting the unknown, because it is an extremely low-risk way to launch new projects. It also involves only a few simple steps:

Act: Take a smart step toward a goal.

Learn: Evaluate the evidence you've created.

Build: Repeat steps 1 and 2 until you accomplish your goal, realize you can't, or opt to change direction on the basis of new information.

Reading that list, you might think, This is common sense. And it is. Any two-year-old understands the concept of learning through action. So do artists and scientists. Even if you don't know exactly where you're going, you get started. You make right turns and wrong turns, learning more about what the right direction is as you go. You're not flying blind; you're moving forward carefully, eyes wide open. You're alert to any looming danger—or opportunity.

We acknowledge that action before analysis, learning instead of predicting, can be, well, unpredictable—and messy. And we concede that it's antithetical to the way most organizations work. However, in the long term, taking lots of small steps actually reduces risk, which makes such an approach ideal for tackling challenges and getting fledgling initiatives off the ground, particularly in today's skittish corporate environment. And such innovation is critically important not only for companies that want to stay competitive but also for enterprising employees who want to feel fulfilled in their jobs.

First Steps

Research shows that entrepreneurs forecast, plan, and model only when they have to. In Sarasvathy's study, not one subject tried to gather specific information about potential returns or predict an ideal level of investment before getting started. But these weren't reckless leaps of faith. No, these entrepreneurs and others like them tend to move in a safe, low-risk way by taking a series of quick, small, inexpensive steps that follow certain rules. Adapted for managers working within organizations, the rules are:

1. Use the means at hand

Successful entrepreneurs, of course, gather resources before embarking on a new venture. For the first few exploratory steps, however, most simply draw on their own skills, education, experience, and expertise, along with anything helpful their personal and professional contacts might have to offer, quickly and at no, or very little, cost. So instead of jumping through hoops to get multiple approvals and formal funding at your company, simply use the people you know, the budget you have— whatever tangible and reputational resources you can muster by picking up the phone, sending an email, or reaching out to a social media contact.

2. Stay within your acceptable loss

The act-learn-build model is inherently low risk, but that doesn't mean it's risk free. So, with each step, consider how much time and money (your own and your company's) you can afford to lose should the step result in failure. Also think about the cost of not pursuing other opportunities at work in order to focus on your project, and the resulting impact on your professional reputation and the firm's image. Make sure that whatever is at risk could be safely lost.

3. Secure only the commitment you need for the next step

Through the process we're discussing, you'll run into four types of people: those who want to make your project happen, those who will help it happen, those who will let it happen, and those who will keep it from happening. Don't waste time trying to get buy-in from the last two types. Instead of asking, "How do I get everyone committed to my idea?" ask, "What's the *least amount of commitment* I need to act?" Aim for just enough freedom to act in an organization designed to push you back into predictive thinking.

4. Bring along only volunteers

If you've decided to move forward, make sure to invest in the "make it happen" and "help it happen" people. The former should be made up of *only volunteers*—people who share your desire. You can't compel others to innovate; if you try, the first setback will send them running to their "real jobs." After identifying these trusted colleagues, make sure they're committed to the process. "Enrollment" happens when you show your own engagement (inspiring your volunteers), act honestly (giving them a complete picture of your plan and presenting both good news and bad), and demonstrate a willingness to collaborate (immediately offering them real work to do).

5. Link your move to a business imperative, and produce early results

This is essential to creating momentum and winning over those in the "help it happen" category—especially your boss. Show how even your first step could make a difference in the world immediately around you, and build out from there. If your boss thinks it won't work, find out why, and see if you agree. If she's hesitant because your proposed step exceeds her acceptable loss, or her boss's, suggest a less significant move.

6. Manage expectations

Don't overpromise. Don't make any big launch announcements. Explain that you're just taking an exploratory step to generate evidence that will inform the direction of the next one.

To see how this process works in practice, consider the experience of Mary Jo Cook and Suzanne Sengelmann, job-share partners and vice presidents in Clorox's laundry and home care division. As committed environmentalists and mothers of small children, Cook and Sengelmann liked natural products and wanted their employer to start producing them. But at the time, when "green" offerings accounted for only 1% of their industry's sales, it was a hard case to make with the predictive analysis that Clorox typically used to identify new business opportunities. The company hadn't launched a major new brand in 20 years—much less tried to break into a small, new market with high barriers to entry. Still, Cook and Sengelmann suspected the category could be a fruitful one and had a strong personal desire to investigate it. (See the sidebar "Why Desire Matters.") So, even as they worked on extensions of Clorox's established, chemical-based products to satisfy the requirements of their job, they gave themselves a new, under-the-radar mandate—develop an effective, marketable, green cleaner—and began to pursue it with smart steps.

At first they simply "played around at home" with products already on the market, and then traded notes on how effective the products were. They also reached out to working-mom colleagues, including Sumi Cate in research and development, whose team was already experimenting with biodegradable plant- and mineral-derived formulas. She was their first "volunteer."

At the time, many people at Clorox were worried that a green line would diminish the brand's reputation for effectiveness, generate paltry profits, and, worse, draw unwelcome attention to the toxic ingredients used in its other offerings. So Cook and Sengelmann kept their interest relatively quiet. But it eventually caught the attention of the company's new-ventures group, which asked them to evaluate an existing European cleaner the group had scouted. The two women and the few volunteers they had by then recruited tried it in their own homes, while Cate's team tested the formulation. Unfortunately, the results were disappointing; the cleaner didn't work well enough to be a Clorox product. But Cook and Sengelmann now had a stronger link to a business imperative—

WHY DESIRE MATTERS

It doesn't make sense to venture into the unknown unless it's for something you care about.

Desire motivates you to act, enables you to persist, and makes you more creative when confronted with obstacles. That doesn't mean you have to have a big idea or a grand passion, at least not at first. Most entrepreneurs begin with a simple interest in a market, product, or service—an itch they need to scratch—and pursue it because it feels satisfying or because they think it might lead to something that does.

Very few of us work at places that are like the early days of Google, where the business model is open, and pet projects are expected to take up 20% of employees' time. Consider the goals of your company, your division, and your boss, and then figure out whether you can link them to what you care about. If you have just been handed a new company initiative, look for something in it that excites you—even if it's just the project's potential to boost your career. If you can't find that connection, consider stepping aside. While it's certainly possible to try the act-learn-build strategy when desire isn't present, it won't be much fun, and your chance of success will be significantly compromised.

namely that a broader set of managers thought a green line could be part of the company's innovation efforts. The trick would be to find an effective one.

They told their bosses about their ambition and explained why it might be a good business for Clorox, but in an informational way that didn't require any sign-offs. That gave them just enough commitment to progress. They also made sure their potential loss during this startup stage was acceptably low: some time and a small percentage of an existing budget, with no threat of diminished reputation because they had made no promises about the green research and they continued to work on other product extensions in the traditional Clorox mold.

After a year, the R&D team finally found a formula that was 99% free of petrochemicals and that worked as well as the company's chemical-based products. But Cook and Sengelmann still had work to do. At that point they could have reverted to extensive market study, models, and financial projections to figure out how to package and sell the new line. But they decided that the market was still too new for the customary in-depth analysis and that internal concerns about the riskiness of green offerings were still too great to be overcome without more evidence. So they stuck with small, smart steps.

They added another "volunteer": their colleague Jessica Buttimer, who was not only a marketing specialist but also another young mother and a health enthusiast. And they began to test prototype products with a small group of consumers in California's Bay Area, where Clorox is based, again using their existing budget and simply keeping their bosses informed. The company learned a lot from this low-risk research: Most users rated the products as highly effective, and all were excited to see the Clorox brand on a green line. It didn't change their opinion of the company's other offerings—they already knew those contained chemicals—but it did change their views on the efficacy of natural products: If Clorox was behind an environmentally friendly brand, it must work. Cook and Sengelmann now had early results on which to build.

Build Momentum

When it comes to learning from and building on our actions, serial entrepreneurs do a better job than the rest of us in four ways: First, they move quickly in the face of positive results. If one step works, they immediately execute the next using the rules we've laid out.

Second, they embrace even negative results. They are grateful for surprises, obstacles, and disappointments because unwelcome news often provides the impetus to make a product, service, or business better, or it points to an entirely different opportunity—before too many resources are invested.

Third, they understand when and how to use prediction, even as they're learning by acting. As your initiative progresses and requires more organizational resources, you'll need to forecast where you can forecast, plan where you can plan, and model where you can model—but using the evidence you have created (and hopefully are still creating) through your smart action steps. This new way of thinking should augment, not replace, the way you currently solve problems.

Fourth, entrepreneurs know when to cut their losses and walk away. They recognize when their idea is impossible to execute, that they're incapable of executing it, or that the risks involved in pursuing it exceed their acceptable loss.

Fortunately, in Cook and Sengelmann's case, the smart steps paid off handsomely. They continued to act their way into the future while simultaneously planning Clorox's classic big-product launch. Another "volunteer" supplied connections at the Sierra Club to secure the San Francisco–based environmental group's seal of approval for the new line. Sample products and packaging were placed on store shelves. Low-cost, grassroots, social media–driven marketing initiatives were tried. The result was Green Works, which within a few years grew to a $60 million brand for Clorox.

We've heard similar success stories from managers in other traditional organizations. One example cited by Harvard Business School professor Rosabeth Moss Kanter is the triumph of a group of tech enthusiasts at cookware retailer Williams-Sonoma, who countered their CEO's lack of interest in e-commerce by launching a low-risk pilot site that has since grown into an industry-leading web presence. Another, smaller-scale case study comes from a Whole Foods Market buyer we know whose interest in nutrition prompted him to pitch to his manager the idea of an in-store bar for vitamin-enhanced smoothies. He now personally staffs it once a week, and it's a big sales driver for the store. Each of us has also had recent firsthand experience with entrepreneurial action at work. Here's one quick example from Len: Instead of spending significant time and money to research whether Babson should create a West Coast outpost, his dean simply opened up admissions and discovered enough demand to start one six months later.

This anecdotal evidence suggests that the act-learn-build strategy can and should be espoused not only by entrepreneurs but also by employees working within traditional organizations. It takes just one smart step to get started.

Leonard A. Schlesinger is Baker Foundation Professor at Harvard Business School and was formerly president of Babson College. **Charles F. Kiefer** is the president of Innovation Associates. **Paul B. Brown** is coauthor of *Relevance: The Power to Change Minds and Stay Ahead of the Competition.* He is a longtime contributor to the *New York Times* and a contributing editor to both *The Conference Board Review* and MIT's *Sloan Management Review.*

NOTE

The authors note that a more detailed look at the Clorox venture is found in *The New Entrepreneurial Leader: Developing Leaders Who Shape Social & Economic Opportunity,* by Danna Greenberg, Kate McKone-Sweet, and H. James Wilson (Berrett-Koehler, 2011).

CHAPTER 10

Monitoring and Controlling Your Project

by Raymond Sheen

Unlike processes—where the same people repeatedly perform the same activities—projects often involve unique activities (such as using new technologies, building new buildings, or writing new software) carried out by individuals who may be working together for the first time. So as a project leader, you'll need to actively monitor progress to figure out whether your plan is really bringing the team closer to its objectives.

Adapted from *HBR Guide to Project Management* (product #11184E), Harvard Business Review Press, 2013, pp. 127–134.

When monitoring and controlling a project, you'll follow five basic steps:

1. Track Project Activities

It's important to check in with team members regularly to make sure they're completing their tasks and meeting quality standards. You can do this most effectively through team meetings if everyone works at the same location. However, given how common distributed teams are in today's business environment, it can be difficult to get the entire group together. When that's the case, I conduct separate working sessions with individuals or small groups needed for particular activities. For example, I recently participated in a "live meeting" conference call where engineers from three locations helped prepare a product-development proposal for a customer. If I had created a draft, sent it around for comments, and then tried to integrate all the feedback, it could easily have taken weeks to complete the document. Instead, I had the right engineers reviewing it over the phone for about three hours, until everybody agreed on the wording. After a working session like this, I loop the rest of the team in at a larger group meeting or through email.

I also use "buddy checks" to verify that tasks are done properly. When someone completes an activity, another team member looks at the results. This is not an in-depth technical analysis; it's a quick check to confirm that the person who did the work hasn't accidentally overlooked something or misunderstood the requirements. A team member checking a training plan for a new system, for example, would make certain that all departments in need of training have been included. If possible, have someone who will *use* the results of the activity do the buddy check. When I worked with a medical device company on developing a new product, I had its regulatory department review the design documentation and test data to flag any missing information that would be required later for regulatory submittal. If a team member with a stake in the activity's result is not available, you can do the buddy check yourself—but make it clear that it's not a performance appraisal. It's just one team member looking out for another.

2. Collect Performance Data

A few companies have project management information systems that automatically generate reports. If you have access to one, by all means use it—but also seek out performance data through short *pulse meetings,* where team members share status updates on activities and assess risks, either face-to-face or virtually. I limit these to 10 minutes and discuss only the tasks started or finished since the last meeting. The purpose is to get a quick sense of where things are, not to roll up sleeves. If the team identifies any problems or risks, I resolve them in a separate working session with the appropriate individuals.

I normally pulse projects on a weekly basis, which allows me to track progress adequately and identify problems in time to respond to them. However, when a project is in crisis mode, the "pulse rate" quickens. I once managed a project in which the power system for a new facility failed three days before the building needed to be up and running. An important business objective hinged on that deadline. The team worked around the clock to identify the cause of the failure, replace the destroyed component, and bring the facility back on line. All that would normally have taken two to three months, but we had three days, so I pulsed the project every three hours.

3. Analyze Performance to Determine Whether the Plan Still Holds

Activities seldom go precisely as anticipated. They may take more or less time; they may overrun or underrun the budget. A departure from your plan isn't a problem unless it's likely to compromise the team's objectives. On one project, I had an engineer report at a pulse meeting that a new mold would be two weeks late. But since the mold wasn't on our critical path and we had nearly six weeks of slack time in that portion of the schedule, the team didn't need to take special action. If the late deliverable had put us in danger of missing an important goal, I would have called a meeting with the appropriate team members to figure out a solution.

This is the time when careful project planning pays dividends. Knowing the critical path will help you decide which issues warrant a schedule change. If you've identified risks up front that could undermine your objectives, you can more easily recognize which snags are threats to the project's success. Having estimated each activity's duration and costs and carefully noted any uncertainties, you'll be able to distinguish between variances that aren't a big deal and those that suggest larger underlying problems.

When a plan does need revising, you may have to extend the end date, apply budget reserves, remove deliverables from the project's scope, or even cancel the project. On one software development project I oversaw, we had an excessively "buggy" first release. Before trying to fix the software, I quickly checked the requirements document and realized that the developers were using an out-of-date version. We had to reschedule the software development task for that module, causing us to delay project completion by about a month, but the change clearly needed to be made.

4. Report Progress to Your Stakeholders

Some project managers and team members perceive *stakeholder reviews*—which involve preparing reports and conducting progress meetings—as wasted effort because they take time away from other activities. However, if managed properly, these reviews propel a project toward success. There are three types: management reviews, tollgate reviews, and technical reviews. For all three, record and circulate action items, and keep meeting minutes in the project file for future reference.

The purpose of the *management review* is to manage risk. Stakeholders may examine several projects at a time to see if the portfolio as a whole will generate the desired business performance and to identify systemic weaknesses. They'll look at individual projects on their own merits as well. Such reviews are normally held at regular intervals—monthly, for instance. When conducting them, keep in mind that your stakeholders care about reaching business goals, not about following the team's day-to-day activities. I recently attended a review where the project leader spent nearly 30 minutes describing technical designs the team was considering and test-ing, which only bored and frustrated the stakeholders. Instead, he should have spent five minutes telling them the project was on schedule (it was), that the team had made progress on its technical analysis (it had), and that no new risks had been identified.

Creating a *project dashboard* is a great way to summa-rize your objectives and show stakeholders whether the project, as currently planned and managed, will achieve them. (You can break it down into components such as schedule, cost, and performance.) This is often called a *stoplight chart,* since it usually indicates activity statuses in red, yellow, and green. Most companies have a standard format to help senior managers quickly and efficiently assess progress and risks on many projects. When using color coding, make sure everyone understands exactly what each color means. For example, do you list all in-complete tasks in red? Or are some of them green, be-cause the plan for completion is approved and underway?

When you need to report bad news in a management review, always couch it in terms of risks to project ob-jectives. Explain how certain task delays will prevent the team from realizing project goals on time, for instance, or how a resource shortage will reduce the rigor of an ac-tivity and thus the quality of its deliverable. When you present problems, also give options for responding to them and discuss the risks associated with each solution. The stakeholders will decide which risks they want the business to take.

The *tollgate review* (also called the *stage-gate review,* or *phase-gate review*) is a decision meeting, not a sta-tus check. It's used when a business plans and executes projects in discrete phases. In it, the project team summarizes the results of the preceding phase and presents a plan for the next phase. The stakeholders assess the plan, options, and risks, and then decide whether to approve, redirect, or cancel the project. If they say to proceed to the next phase, they also provide the team with the necessary resources, including funding.

At a *technical review* (sometimes referred to as a *peer review*), an independent team of experts—internal or external consultants, say, or representatives from a regulatory agency—provides an in-depth analysis of project results. The purpose is to ensure that team members did the work accurately, completely, and to the right quality standard. Stakeholders may give a stamp of approval at this time: If the team has successfully completed one phase of the project, it can now proceed to a tollgate review for approval to begin the next phase.

5. Manage Changes to the Plan

When revising a plan, you may make major changes or just minor tweaks that will allow the team to meet its objectives.

If you propose major changes to your stakeholders, spell out the costs and risks of adopting them and those of sticking with the original plan. A defense contractor that I work with was asked by the Air Force to improve performance of a weapon-system component. After the Air Force reviewed the proposed options (which included costs, risks, and schedules) and selected one, the contractor synchronized updates to design documentation, manufacturing processes, supplier contracts, the project schedule, and the budget so the transition would be as seamless as possible. When making such large-scale revisions, record them (along with the rationale) on some type of change log in the project records. You can use your normal project-planning processes and techniques to revise your plan. Send the new plan to your team members, and explain any changes that affect them.

Minor changes may come up as you're implementing a contingency plan or working out details of a portion of the project that was planned only at a high level. The project team can usually manage these on its own, without seeking stakeholder approval, unless the changes will directly affect stakeholders or their departments.

As you're monitoring your project, remember that meeting your objectives trumps everything else. Don't get hung up on compliance with the original plan. In my experience, almost every project plan must be revised at some point—especially when you're developing new products or systems, because what you learn in the early stages sheds light on how later-stage tasks should take shape. Don't be afraid to change course if it will bring you within reach of your goals.

———————

Raymond Sheen, PMP, is the president of Product & Process Innovation, a consulting firm specializing in project management, product development, and process improvement. He is the author, with Amy Gallo, of the *HBR Guide to Building Your Business Case* (Harvard Business Review Press, 2015).

CHAPTER 11

Building a Transformative Team

by Nathan Furr, Kyle Nel, and Thomas Zoëga Ramsøy

An all-star team is making headway with a new initiative that could alter the future of the organization. Spirits are optimistic, and the team is successfully maneuvering through new, yet very promising, territory. Then, the results begin taking longer than anticipated to prove, and after too much time spent outside of their comfort zones, the team of high-achieving employees can't seem to execute within the uncertain environment.

Adapted from "If Your Innovation Effort Isn't Working, Look at Who's on the Team," on hbr.org, November 9, 2018 (product #H04N87).

The team's outlook shifts, and it becomes clear that the group will not be able to weather the storm of uncertainty needed to realize this new organizational opportunity.

How could such a capable team fail?

At the heart of many organizations is a deeper problem that blocks transformation: product/function organizational structure. This structure works in well-understood environments, where maximizing delivery of a product or service is the goal, but transformative projects require the organization to return to a more malleable state. This challenge requires teams that are formed through a rematching of resources and employee capabilities.

Transformation-capable teams are made up of people who not only are high performers, but have a unique balance of skills and mindsets that allows them to sustain focus, agility, and optimism in the face of uncertainty for prolonged periods of time. Ultimately, not all top-performing employees are equipped for this.

In our book, *Leading Transformation: How to Take Charge of Your Company's Future*, we highlight certain capabilities to search for and cultivate while building a transformative team. Specifically, there are three unique characteristics that will play critical roles as a team takes on a breakthrough initiative.

Negative Capability: Being Comfortable with Uncertainty

The term "negative capability" was coined by the poet John Keats when describing writers like Shakespeare who were able to work within uncertainty and doubt. Keats was describing the ability to accept not having an immediate answer and to remain willing to explore how something may evolve before there is a clear outcome.

In the modern context, negative capability can be thought of as the ability to be comfortable with uncertainty, even to entertain it, rather than to become so anxious by its presence that you have to prematurely race to a more certain, yet suboptimal, conclusion. Whereas many people cannot stand the fuzziness of uncertainty, those who demonstrate negative capabilities can facilitate the exploration of new terrain and the discovery of an adjacent possible opportunity.

Individuals with negative capability remain curious and focused even when your project is far from the end goal. Chances are, they will even find this point of the project enthralling, rather than overwhelming, which is exactly what you want. They will also be able to suspend judgment about an end result and stay open to many possible outcomes, rather than become fixed early on to one version of success.

Chaos Pilots: Leading and Executing in Unfamiliar Territory

In 1991, Danish politician and social worker Uffe Elbæk took out a $100,000 personal loan to open an unusual business school called Kaospilot. The vision of the business school was inspired by a previous project of Elbæk's, where he observed a new skill set in students for navigating uncertain problems and saw the opportunity to teach these skills to business leaders who needed to do the same. *Chaos pilot* is a perfect label for a specific persona needed on a transformative team.

Chaos pilots are people who can creatively lead a project through uncertainty. They have negative capability, but they also have other critical skills, such as the ability to create structure within chaos and take action. Leaders who are chaos pilots are able to drive a team forward on a project even as the environment around them fluctuates.

Although it may sound glamorous to be such a person, being a chaos pilot is hard—they are the colleagues working on ambiguous projects and frequently getting beat up in the process. People who aren't capable of being chaos pilots quickly flounder when the environment around the project gets shaky.

Chaos pilots often care more about creating meaningful change than about climbing a corporate ladder or getting another star on their charts. Finding chaos pilots to join you can be challenging and requires observation and experimentation, though there are a few fertile places to look for good candidates.

For example, look for people who are getting mixed performance reviews, but who are still highly prized by the organization. Often, these people are getting mixed reviews because they make those around them uncomfortable—as the potential candidates often challenge the status quo—but they continue to succeed because they perform so well.

Divergent Thinking, Convergent Action, and Influential Communication

Finally, there are three neuropsychological traits to seek while building a transformative team. These three traits—divergent thinking, convergent action, and influential communication—all play a crucial role for success in innovation and transformation. While many individuals hold one or two of these skills, finding a person with all three is more challenging, yet optimal.

The first of the three, divergent thinking, is the ability to uniquely connect new information, ideas, and concepts that are usually held far apart. People with this skill can match dissimilar concepts in novel and meaningful ways and uncover new opportunities that others may overlook.

Convergent action, the second trait, is the ability to execute on these new ideas in order to create something tangible. Though many people can come up with great ideas, it is often those with convergent action who will move that new concept from idea to product. Last, having the ability to communicate ideas in a coherent, compelling, and influential way is paramount. This trait will inspire other leaders and decision makers to believe, support, and act on a novel idea or opportunity.

Similar to how many transformative business opportunities are found in unlikely places, the same is true about where you may find the best-suited team members to drive forward a promising new initiative.

Each organizational project represents a moment of potential transformation, and each successful project helps an organization self-correct away from becoming a calloused machine executing on routine and instead become what it needs to survive: a malleable organization capable of capturing new opportunities.

Nathan Furr is a strategy professor at INSEAD. **Kyle Nel** is the CEO and cofounder of Uncommon Partners, a behavioral transformation consultancy, and the former executive director of Lowe's Innovation Labs. **Thomas Zoëga Ramsøy** is the founder and CEO of Neurons Inc. They are coauthors of *Leading Transformation: How to Take Charge of Your Company's Future* (Harvard Business Review Press, 2018).

CHAPTER 12

Teamwork
on the Fly

by Amy C. Edmondson

If you watched the Beijing Olympic Games, you probably marveled at the Water Cube: that magnificent 340,000-square-foot box framed in steel and covered with semitransparent, ecoefficient blue bubbles. Formally named the Beijing National Aquatics Center, the Water Cube hosted swimming and diving events, could hold 17,000 spectators, won prestigious engineering and design awards, and cost an estimated 10.2 billion yuan. The structure was the joint effort of global design and engineering company Arup, PTW Architects, the China State Construction Engineering Corporation (CSCEC),

---

Adapted from *Harvard Business Review*, April 2012 (product #R1204D).

China Construction Design International, and dozens of contractors and consultants. The goal was clear: Build an iconic structure to reflect Chinese culture, integrate with the site, and minimize energy consumption—on time and within budget. But how to do all that was less clear.

Ultimately, Tristram Carfrae, an Arup structural engineer based in Sydney, corralled dozens of people from 20 disciplines and four countries to win the competition and deliver the building. This required more than traditional project management. Success depended on bridging dramatically different national, organizational, and occupational cultures to collaborate in fluid groupings that emerged and dissolved in response to needs that were identified as the work progressed.

The Water Cube was an unusual endeavor, but the strategy employed to complete it—a strategy I call *teaming*—epitomizes the new era of business. Teaming is teamwork on the fly: a pickup basketball game rather than plays run by a team that has trained as a unit for years. It's a way to gather experts in temporary groups to solve problems they're encountering for the first and perhaps only time. Think of clinicians in an emergency room, who convene quickly to solve a specific patient problem and then move on to address other cases with different colleagues, compared with a surgical team that performs the same procedure under highly controlled conditions day after day. When companies need to accomplish something that hasn't been done before, and might not be done again, traditional team structures aren't practical. It's just not possible to identify the right skills and knowledge in advance and to trust that circumstances will not change. Under those conditions, a leader's emphasis has to shift from composing and managing teams to inspiring and enabling teaming.

Stable teams of people who have learned over time to work well together can be powerful tools. But given the speed of change, the intensity of market competition, and the unpredictability of customers' needs today, there often isn't enough time to build that kind of team. Instead, organizations increasingly must bring together not only their own far-flung employees from various disciplines and divisions but also external specialists and stakeholders, only to disband them when they've achieved their goal or when a new opportunity arises. More and more people in nearly every industry and type of company are now working on multiple teams that vary in duration, have a constantly shifting membership, and pursue moving targets. Product design, patient care, strategy development, pharmaceutical research, and rescue operations are just a few of the domains in which teaming is essential.

This evolution of teamwork presents serious challenges. In fact, it can lead to chaos. But employees and organizations that learn how to team well—by embracing several project management and team leadership principles—can reap important benefits. Teaming helps individuals acquire knowledge, skills, and networks. And it lets companies accelerate the delivery of current products and services while responding quickly to new opportunities. Teaming is a way to get work done while figuring out how to do it better; it's executing and learning at the same time.

From Teams to Teaming

The stable project teams we grew up with still work beautifully in many contexts. By pulling together the right people with the right combination of skills and training and giving them time to build trust, companies can accomplish big things. For instance, traditional teams at Simmons Bedding Company in the early 2000s achieved a major turnaround by driving waste out of operations, energizing sales, and building better relationships with dealers. In those teams, membership was clearly defined, each group knew which part of the operation it was responsible for, and no one had to do fundamentally new types of work. These stable teams left a trail of positive indicators, including savings of $21 million in operational costs without layoffs in the first year alone; increased sales and customer satisfaction; and dramatically improved employee morale. But Simmons had what many companies today lack: reasonably stable customer preferences, purely domestic operations, and no significant boundaries that had to be crossed to get the job done.

Situations that call for teaming are, by contrast, complex and uncertain, full of unexpected events that require rapid changes in course. No two projects are alike, so people must get up to speed quickly on brand-new topics, again and again. Because solutions can come from anywhere, team members do, too. As a result, teaming requires people to cross boundaries, which can be risky. Experts from different functions—operating with their own jargon, norms, and knowledge—often clash. People who aren't from the same division or organization can have competing values and priorities. When junior and senior staff members from different divisions are paired, reporting structures and hierarchies often silence dissent. On global teams, time zone differences and electronic correspondence can give rise to miscommunication and logistical snafus. And because the work relationships are temporary, investing the time to grow accustomed to new colleagues' work styles, strengths, and weaknesses isn't possible.

Disagreements were plentiful in designing the Water Cube, given the need for intense collaboration across boundaries. Early on, two architecture firms—one Chinese and one Australian—each developed a design concept. One was a wave-shaped structure, and the other was an eroded rectangular form. A participant recalled tension between what felt like two camps. Another added, "It was like two design processes were going on at the same time. One team was working secretly on its idea, and the other architects were doing their own thing."

Consider also a geographically distributed product development team I studied in a high-tech materials company. Working to develop a custom polymer for a Japanese manufacturer's new-product launch, the group nearly broke down over conflicting cultural norms about customer relationships. One team member, a U.S.-based marketing expert, wanted data on the manufacturer's market strategy to assess the longer-term opportunity for the polymer; she was deeply frustrated by a Japanese team member's failure to fulfill her request. In turn, the Japanese team member, an engineer, thought the U.S.

marketer was pushy and unsupportive. She knew that the customer had not yet established a strategy for the product and that demanding more information at this stage in the nascent relationship would cause the customer to "lose face."

At the same company, another team of seven experts spread across five facilities on three continents was trying to develop a different polymer on an aggressive timetable. In spite of its combined knowledge, the group reached a dead end in an effort to source a specialized compound. One member eventually found a colleague from outside the formal team who could produce it. In technologically and scientifically complex projects like this one, teaming occurs not just across the boundaries it was designed to span but also across boundaries between projects, when colleagues with expertise and goodwill help out.

As these brief examples illustrate, teaming involves both technical and interpersonal challenges. It therefore falls to leaders to draw on best practices of project management (to plan and execute in a complex and changing environment) and team leadership (to foster collaboration in shifting groups that will be inherently prone to conflict). This is the hardware and the software of teaming. Let's tackle the hardware first.

The Hardware

To facilitate effective teaming, leaders need to manage the technical issues of *scoping* out the challenge, lightly *structuring* the boundaries, and *sorting* tasks for execution. A classic error is assuming that everything a team does has to be collaborative. Instead, input and inter-action should be used as needed so that not all tasks become team encounters, which are time consuming. Another error is subjecting highly uncertain initiatives to traditional project management tools that cope with complexity by dividing work into predictable phases such as initiation, planning, execution, completion, and monitoring. The hardware of teaming modifies those tools to enable execution during, rather than after, learn-ing and planning.

Scoping

The first step in any teaming scenario is to draw a line in the (shifting) sand by scoping out the challenge, de-termining what expertise is needed, tapping collabora-tors, and outlining roles and responsibilities. Leaders of the Water Cube project, for example, started by identi-fying a handful of Pacific Rim firms that were capable of state-of-the-art engineering and design and willing to work together. In other organizations, this scouting ac-tivity might involve lateral and vertical searches through the hierarchy to identify people with relevant expertise. When a team is already assembled, scoping includes figuring out what additional resources are needed, as occurred in the second polymer team, or which team members can be freed up over time to join other groups. Successful scoping articulates the best possible current definition of the work and acknowledges that the defini-tion will evolve along with the project.

Structuring

The second step is to offer some structure—figurative scaffolding—to help the team function effectively. In building, a scaffold is a light, temporary structure that supports the process of construction. For improvisational, interdependent work carried out by a shifting mix of participants, some structuring can help the group by establishing boundaries and targets. Scaffolding in a teaming situation could include a list of team members that contains pertinent biographical and professional information; a shared radio frequency, chat room, or intranet; visits to teammates' facilities; or temporary shared office space. The use of "shirts" and "skins" to designate sides in a pickup basketball game is a kind of scaffold, as is a quick briefing at the launch of a rescue mission that assigns, say, groups of four people, each with a different role, to head in three different directions. The objective of structuring is to make it easier for teaming partners to coordinate and communicate—face-to-face or virtually.

Melissa Valentine, a doctoral candidate at Harvard University, and I recently looked at the use of figurative scaffolds in emergency rooms, where fast-paced teaming has life-or-death consequences. In this setting, physicians, nurses, and technicians with constantly varying schedules depend on one another to make good patient care decisions and execute them flawlessly in real time. More often than not, people scheduled on the same shift do not have long-standing work relationships and may not even know one another's names. Valentine and I found several hospitals that were experimenting with a system to make ad hoc collaboration easier by dividing ERs into subsections ("pods") incorporating a preset mix of roles (such as an attending physician, three nurses, a resident, and an intern) into which clinicians slide when they come to work. As a result, the teaming arrangement for each shift is established early on, which reduces coordination time, boosts accountability, improves operational efficiency, and shortens patient waits.

Temporary colocation is a common type of scaffold for high-priority, short-term projects in corporate settings. Motorola used this for one of the most successful product launches in history: the RAZR mobile phone. Battling fierce global competition in 2003, the company set out to create the thinnest phone ever in record time. Roger Jellicoe, an electrical engineer, led the project, in which 20 engineers and other experts from various groups and locations temporarily worked side by side in an otherwise unremarkable facility an hour from Chicago. The resulting product, introduced in 2004, was a stunning market success: More than 110 million RAZRs were sold in the first four years.

Sorting

The third step is the conscious prioritizing of tasks according to the degree of interdependence among individuals. As the organizational theorist James Thompson noted a half century ago, organizations exist to combine people's efforts. Combining, or interdependence, can take three forms: pooled, sequential, or reciprocal. *Pooled* interdependence was the very essence of the industrial era—breaking work down into small tasks that could be done and monitored individually, without input from others. To the extent that such work exists in current projects, there's flexibility in when and where it gets done. But most tasks now require some degree of interaction among individuals or subgroups.

Sequential interdependence characterizes tasks that need input (information, material, or both) from someone else. The assembly line is the classic example: Unless the guy upstream does his part, I cannot do mine. Teaming situations are full of these tasks; they must be scheduled carefully to avoid delays. Effective teaming streamlines handoffs between sequential tasks to avoid wasted time and miscommunication. Too often, people focus on their own part of the work and assume that if others do likewise, that will be sufficient for good performance.

The management of tasks involving *reciprocal* interdependence—work that calls for back-and-forth communication and mutual adjustment—is most critical to successful teaming. Because it's often difficult for people in cross-functional, fluid groups to reach consensus, these tasks tend to become bottlenecks. They should therefore be prioritized. It's crucial that leaders specify points when individuals or subgroups must gather—literally or virtually—to coordinate upcoming decisions and resources or to analyze and solve problems.

One factor that distinguished the design and construction of the Water Cube from most large-scale building projects—in which different tasks are performed sequentially by different disciplines—was that all the experts came together at the beginning to brainstorm and consider the implications of various design ideas. This decision about process deliberately converted tradition-ally sequential activities into reciprocal ones. The result was greater complexity and more need for coordination but also better design, less waste, quicker completion, and lower cost. One outcome was the radical decision to use ethylene tetrafluoroethylene (ETFE), a material that had been developed for space exploration but never used in a major building. Its unique properties solved several acoustic, structural, and lighting problems, and although the choice initially appeared risky, Arup engineers used the latest computer modeling software to confirm the safety of ETFE for their purposes and to communicate their thinking to the Chinese authorities.

Of course not all tasks in the Water Cube project re-quired reciprocal interdependence. Expert subgroups had many independent tasks, such as fire safety analyses and certain technical drawings. But for interdependent work, groups had to coordinate across what the com-pany called "interfaces." Carfrae and his colleagues di-vided the entire project into "volumes" (separable parts) on the basis of areas of interdependence and assigned subteams to carry them out. When issues required co-ordination across volumes, interface coordination meet-ings were held—for just the relevant parties—to manage the structural, organizational, or procedural boundaries. In this way, the project eliminated mistakes that might otherwise occur at such boundaries—saving materials, costs, and headaches.

The Software

The hardware of teaming rarely works smoothly unless the software is thoughtfully managed as well. (See the sidebar "The Behaviors of Successful Teaming.") One challenge of any kind of teamwork is that people working together are more vulnerable to the effects of others' decisions and actions than people working independently. Stable teams overcome this by giving members time to get to know and trust one another, which makes it easier to speak up, listen closely, and interact fluidly. But constantly shifting relationships heighten the challenge. The software of teaming asks people to get comfortable with a new way of working rather than with a new set of colleagues. This new way of working requires them to act as if they trust one another—even though they don't. Of course they don't; they don't yet know one another. Leaders have at their disposal four software tools: emphasizing purpose, building psychological safety, embracing failure, and putting conflict to work.

Emphasizing purpose

Articulating what's at stake is a basic leadership tool for motivation in almost any setting, but it's particularly important in contexts that require teaming. Purpose is fundamentally about shared values; it answers the question why we (this company, this project) exist, which can galvanize even the most diverse, amorphous team. Emphasizing purpose is necessary even when the purpose is obvious, such as in the historic 70-day rescue operation of 33 Chilean miners in 2010. Andre Sougarret, the senior engineer at the Codelco mining company who led the complex rescue, constantly reminded the dozens of engineers and geologists teaming with him about the human lives they were trying to save. This helped experts from

THE BEHAVIORS OF SUCCESSFUL TEAMING

Speaking Up

Communicating honestly and directly with others by asking questions, acknowledging errors, raising issues, and explaining ideas

Experimenting

Taking an iterative approach to action that recognizes the novelty and uncertainty inherent in interactions between individuals and in the possibilities and plans they develop

Reflecting

Observing, questioning, and discussing processes and outcomes on a consistent basis—daily, weekly, monthly— that reflects the rhythm of the work

Listening Intently

Working hard to understand the knowledge, expertise, ideas, and opinions of others

Integrating

Synthesizing different facts and points of view to create new possibilities disparate disciplines, companies, and countries quickly resolve disagreements and support one another instead of competing to come up with the idea that would save the day. Jellicoe and the Motorola RAZR team emphasized producing a groundbreaking product that would be beautiful as well as practical, while the polymer developers had a mandate to satisfy their customers' needs as quickly and effectively as they could.

Building psychological safety

In fast-paced, cross-disciplinary, cross-border teaming situations, it's not necessarily easy for people to rapidly share relevant information about their ideas and expertise. Some people worry about what others will think of them. Some fear that they will be less valuable if they give away what they know. Others are reluctant to show off. Even receiving knowledge can be difficult if it feels like an admission of weakness.

Because these vital interpersonal exchanges don't always happen spontaneously, leaders must facilitate them by creating a climate of psychological safety in which it's expected that people will speak up and disagree. A basic way to create such a climate is to model the behaviors on which teaming depends: asking thoughtful questions, acknowledging ignorance about a topic or area of expertise, and conveying awareness of one's own fallibility. Leaders who act this way make it safer for everyone else to do so. To establish a psychologically safe environment for the rescue operation in Chile, Sougarret shielded everyone involved from the media, asked questions and listened carefully to people regardless of rank, and demonstrated deep interest in new ideas about how to save the miners. In the Water Cube project, Carfrae created what team members referred to as a "safe design environment" by reinforcing the need to experiment with wild ideas.

Embracing failure

Teaming necessarily leads to failures, even on the way to extraordinary successes. These failures provide essential information that guides the next steps, creating an imperative to learn from them.

In teaming situations, leaders must ensure that all participants get over their natural desire to avoid the embarrassment and loss of confidence associated with making mistakes. The RAZR team confronted failure when, despite long working hours, it missed its ambitious deadline and the associated holiday sales. Fully supported by senior management, the team launched a few months later, and the phone's sales still surpassed expectations. The first polymer team described above undertook a series of experiments that went nowhere and ultimately brought in some specialists, confident that those colleagues would not think less of them. Teaming is needed for just those kinds of situations— when the people responsible for implementing solutions are not necessarily the ones who can come up with them.

Putting conflict to work

When teaming occurs across diverse cultures, priorities, or values, progress-thwarting conflicts are common—even when leaders have done all the right things.

To move forward, all parties must be pushed to consider the degree to which their positions reflect not just facts but also personal values and biases, to explain how they have arrived at their views, and to express interest in one another's analytic journeys. In this way, people can put conflict to good use.

As Chris Argyris wrote in the HBR article "Teaching Smart People How to Learn," learning from conflict requires us to balance our natural tendency toward advocacy (explaining, communicating, teaching) with a less spontaneous behavior: inquiry (expressions of curiosity followed by genuine listening). A useful discipline for leaders is to force moments of reflection, asking themselves and then others, "Is this the only way to see the situation? What might I be missing?" Such exploration—even in the face of deadlines—is critical to successful teaming. In fact, in my research and consulting I've found that "taking the time" to do this actually takes less time than allowing conflicts to follow their natural course.

Conflict can feel like a failure. It can be frustrating not to see eye-to-eye with collaborators, but differences of perspective are a core reason for teamwork in the first place, and resolving them effectively gives rise to new opportunities. Instead of parting ways when they disagreed about the design for the Olympic aquatics center, the Chinese and Australian designers came up with a brand-new concept that excited both sides. Would either of their original design concepts have won the competition? We can't answer that, but the new, shared solution—the Water Cube—was spectacular. Project leaders facilitated this successful outcome by assigning those rare specialists who had deep familiarity with both Chinese and Western culture to spend time in each other's firms helping to bridge differences in language, norms, practices, and expectations.

Challenges Bring Benefits

Having studied the evolution of teamwork for 20 years, I believe that teaming is not just something individuals and companies have to do now but something they should want to do now, because it's an important driver of personal and organizational development.

When managed effectively, teaming can generate not only amazing short-term results, as illustrated by the RAZR and the Water Cube, but also long-term dividends. (See table 12-1, "The Rewards of Teaming.") Organizations that learn to team well become nimbler and more innovative. They are able to solve complex, cross-disciplinary problems, align divisions and employees by developing stronger and more-unified corporate cultures, deliver a wide variety of products and services, and manage unexpected events. Teaming helps companies execute even as they learn on multiple fronts, which in turn leads to improved execution.

Individuals also benefit from serial teaming, developing broader knowledge, better interpersonal skills, a bigger network of potential collaborators, and a better understanding of their company and the different cultures at work in it. In a study of product development teams, my colleagues and I found that people who had worked on teams with greater task novelty and product

TABLE 12-1

The rewards of teaming

The most challenging attributes of teaming can also yield big organizational and individual benefits.

Multiple functions must work together	People are geographically dispersed	Relationships are temporary	No two projects are alike	The work can be uncertain and chaotic
Challenges				
Conflict can arise among people with differing values, norms, jargon, and expertise.	Time zone differences and electronic communication present logistical hurdles.	People may not have time to build trust and mutual understanding.	Individuals must get up to speed on brand-new topics quickly, again and again.	Fluid situations require constant communication and coordination.
Benefits				
ORGANIZATIONAL Innovation from combining skills and perspectives Ability to solve cross-disciplinary problems	*ORGANIZATIONAL* Greater alignment across divisions Better diffusion of the company's culture	*ORGANIZATIONAL* More shared experience among colleagues Greater camaraderie across the company	*ORGANIZATIONAL* Ability to meet changing customer needs	*ORGANIZATIONAL* Ability to manage unexpected events
INDIVIDUAL Boundary-spanning skills Understanding of other disciplines Broader perspective on the business	*INDIVIDUAL* Familiarity with people in different locations Deeper understanding of different cultures and of the organization's operations	*INDIVIDUAL* Interpersonal skills Extensive network of collaborators	*INDIVIDUAL* Flexibility and agility Ability to import ideas from one context to another	*INDIVIDUAL* Project management skills Experimentation skills

complexity, more-diverse colleagues, and more bound-
ary spanning learned more than people on teams that
faced fewer of those challenges.

The multinational food company Group Danone believes so strongly in the power of teaming that the company has institutionalized it in the form of Networking
Attitude, a program initiated by the executives Franck
Mougin and Benedikt Benenati. It encourages ad hoc
projects involving employees spread across hundreds of
business units that previously operated independently,
with little or no cross-pollination. Using a mix of face-
to-face "knowledge marketplaces" and electronically me-
diated discussions, managers with an interest in a particular issue, brand, or problem can find partners with
whom to share practices and launch new initiatives. An
internal report featured stories of 33 practices transferred across sites, from which the company expects new
teams and projects to bubble up. One initiative involved
a dessert Danone Brazil helped Danone France launch in
under three months in response to a competitor's move;
it became a €20 million business. The company now has
more than 60 new "networks"—porous communities of
teaming colleagues—around the globe. Networking Attitude was designed to produce business successes, and
it did. But, just as important, it shifted a culture of local-
ized, hierarchical decision making to one of horizontal
collaboration.

Teaming is more chaotic than traditional teamwork,
but it is here to stay. Projects increasingly require information and process sophistication from many fields.
And managers are dependent on all kinds of specialists

to make decisions and get work done. To excel in a complex and uncertain business environment, people need to work together in new and unpredictable ways. That's why successful teaming starts with an embrace of the unknown and a commitment to learning that drives employees to absorb, and sometimes create, new knowledge while executing.

Amy C. Edmondson is the Novartis Professor of Leadership and Management at Harvard Business School. She is the author of *The Fearless Organization: Creating Psychological Safety in the Workplace for Learning, Innovation, and Growth* and a coauthor of *Building the Future: Big Teaming for Audacious Innovation*.

CHAPTER 13

Why Good Projects Fail Anyway

by Nadim F. Matta and Ronald N. Ashkenas

Big projects fail at an astonishing rate. Whether major technology installations, postmerger integrations, or new growth strategies, these efforts consume tremendous resources over months or even years. Yet as study after study has shown, they frequently deliver disappointing returns—by some estimates, in fact, well over half the time. And the toll they take is not just financial. These failures demoralize employees who have labored diligently to complete their share of the work. One middle manager at a top pharmaceutical company told us,

Reprinted from *Harvard Business Review*, September 2003 (product #R0309H).

"I've been on dozens of task teams in my career, and I've never actually seen one that produced a result."

The problem is, the traditional approach to project management shifts the project teams' focus away from the end result toward developing recommendations, new technologies, and partial solutions. The intent, of course, is to piece these together into a blueprint that will achieve the ultimate goal, but when a project involves many people working over an extended period of time, it's very hard for managers planning it to predict all the activities and work streams that will be needed. Unless the end product is very well understood, as it is in highly technical engineering projects such as building an airplane, it's almost inevitable that some things will be left off the plan. And even if all the right activities have been anticipated, they may turn out to be difficult, or even impossible, to knit together once they're completed.

Managers use project plans, timelines, and budgets to reduce what we call "execution risk"—the risk that designated activities won't be carried out properly—but they inevitably neglect these two other critical risks—the "white space risk" that some required activities won't be identified in advance, leaving gaps in the project plan, and the "integration risk" that the disparate activities won't come together at the end. So project teams can execute their tasks flawlessly, on time and under budget, and yet the overall project may still fail to deliver the intended results.

We've worked with hundreds of teams over the past 20 years, and we've found that by designing complex projects differently, managers can reduce the likelihood that critical activities will be left off the plan and increase the odds that all the pieces can be properly integrated at the end. The key is to inject into the overall plan a series of miniprojects—what we call *rapid-results initiatives*—each staffed with a team responsible for a version of the hoped-for overall result in miniature and each designed to deliver its result quickly.

Let's see what difference that would make. Say, for example, your goal is to double sales revenue over two years by implementing a customer relationship management (CRM) system for your sales force. Using a traditional project management approach, you might have one team research and install software packages, another analyze the different ways that the company interacts with customers (email, telephone, and in person, for example), another develop training programs, and so forth. Many months later, however, when you start to roll out the program, you might discover that the salespeople aren't sold on the benefits. So even though they may know how to enter the requisite data into the system, they refuse. This very problem has, in fact, derailed many CRM programs at major organizations.

But consider the way the process might unfold if the project included some rapid-results initiatives. A single team might take responsibility for helping a small number of users—say, one sales group in one region—increase their revenues by 25% within four months. Team members would probably draw on all the activities described above, but to succeed at their goal, the microcosm of the overall goal, they would be forced to find out what, if anything, is missing from their plans as they go forward.

Along the way, they would, for example, discover the salespeople's resistance, and they would be compelled to educate the sales staff about the system's benefits. The team may also discover that it needs to tackle other issues, such as how to divvy up commissions on sales resulting from cross-selling or joint-selling efforts.

When they've ironed out all the kinks on a small scale, their work would then become a model for the next teams, which would either engage in further rapid-results initiatives or roll the system out to the whole organization—but now with a higher level of confidence that the project will have the intended impact on sales revenue. The company would see an early payback on its investment and gain new insights from the team's work, and the team would have the satisfaction of delivering real value.

In the pages that follow, we'll take a close look at rapid-results initiatives, using case studies to show how these projects are selected and designed and how they are managed in conjunction with more traditional project activities.

How Rapid-Results Teams Work

Let's look at an extremely complex project, a World Bank initiative begun in June 2000 that aims to improve the productivity of 120,000 small-scale farmers in Nicaragua by 30% in 16 years. A project of this magnitude entails many teams working over a long period of time, and it crosses functional and organizational boundaries.

They started as they had always done: A team of World Bank experts and their clients in the country (in this case, Ministry of Agriculture officials) spent many months in preparation—conducting surveys, analyzing data, talking to people with comparable experiences in other countries, and so on. Based on their findings, these project strategists, designers, and planners made an educated guess about the major streams of work that would be required to reach the goal. These work streams included reorganizing government institutions that give technical advice to farmers, encouraging the creation of a private-sector market in agricultural support services (such as helping farmers adopt new farming technologies and use improved seeds), strengthening the National Institute for Agricultural Technology (INTA), and establishing an information management system that would help agricultural R&D institutions direct their efforts to the most productive areas of research. The result of all this preparation was a multiyear project plan, a document laying out the work streams in detail.

But if the World Bank had kept proceeding in the traditional way on a project of this magnitude, it would have been years before managers found out if something had been left off the plan or if the various work streams could be integrated—and thus if the project would ultimately achieve its goals. By that time, millions of dollars would have been invested and much time potentially wasted. What's more, even if everything worked according to plan, the project's beneficiaries would have been waiting for years before seeing any payoff from the effort. As it happened, the project activities proceeded on schedule, but a new minister of agriculture came on board two years in and argued that he needed to see results sooner than the plan allowed. His complaint resonated with Norman Piccioni, the World Bank team leader, who was also getting impatient with the project's pace. As he said at the time, "Apart from the minister, the farmers, and me, I'm not sure anyone working on this project is losing sleep over whether farmer productivity will be improved or not."

Over the next few months, we worked with Piccioni to help him and his clients add rapid-results initiatives to the implementation process. They launched five teams, which included not only representatives from the existing work streams but also the beneficiaries of the project, the farmers themselves. The teams differed from traditional implementation teams in three fundamental ways. Rather than being partial, horizontal, and long term, they were results oriented, vertical, and fast. A look at each attribute in turn shows why they were more effective.

Results oriented

As the name suggests, a rapid-results initiative is intentionally commissioned to produce a measurable result, rather than recommendations, analyses, or partial solutions. And even though the goal is on a smaller scale than the overall objective, it is nonetheless challenging. In Nicaragua, one team's goal was to increase Grade A milk production in the Leon municipality from 600 to 1,600 gallons per day in 120 days in 60 small and medium-size producers. Another was to increase pig weight on 30 farms by 30% in 100 days using enhanced corn seed. A third was to secure commitments from private-sector experts to provide technical advice and agricultural support to 150 small-scale farmers in the El Sauce (the dry farming region) within 100 days.

This results orientation is important for three reasons. First, it allows project planners to test whether the activities in the overall plan will add up to the intended result and to alter the plans if need be. Second, it produces real benefits in the short term. Increasing pig weight in 30 farms by 30% in just over three months is useful to those 30 farmers no matter what else happens in the project. And finally, being able to deliver results is more rewarding and energizing for teams than plodding along through partial solutions.

The focus on results also distinguishes rapid-results initiatives from pilot projects, which are used in traditionally managed initiatives only to reduce execution risk. Pilots typically are designed to test a preconceived solution, or means, such as a CRM system, and to work out implementation details before rollout. Rapid-results initiatives, by contrast, are aimed squarely at reducing white space and integration risk.

Vertical

Project plans typically unfold as a series of activities represented on a timeline by horizontal bars. In this context, rapid-results initiatives are vertical. They encompass a slice of several horizontal activities, implemented in tandem in a very short time frame. By using the term "vertical," we also suggest a cross-functional effort, since different horizontal work streams usually include people from different parts of an organization (or even, as in

Nicaragua, different organizations), and the vertical slice brings these people together. This vertical orientation is key to reducing white space and integration risks in the overall effort: Only by uncovering and properly integrating any activities falling in the white space between the horizontal project streams will the team be able to deliver its miniresult. (For a look at the horizontal and vertical work streams in the Nicaragua project, see the sidebar "The World Bank's Project Plan.")

The team working on securing commitments between farmers and technical experts in the dry farming region, for example, had to knit together a broad set of activities. The experts needed to be trained to deliver particular services that the farmers were demanding because they had heard about new ways to increase their productivity through the information management system. That, in turn, was being fed information coming out of INTA's R&D efforts, which were directed toward addressing specific problems the farmers had articulated. So team members had to draw on a number of the broad horizontal activities laid out in the overall project plan and integrate them into their vertical effort. As they did so, they discovered that they had to add activities missing from the original horizontal work streams. Despite the team members' heroic efforts to integrate the ongoing activities, for instance, 80 days into their 100-day initiative, they had secured only half the commitments they were aiming for. Undeterred and spurred on by the desire to accomplish their goal, team members drove through the towns of the region announcing with loudspeakers the availability and benefits of the technical services. Over the following 20 days, the gap to the goal was closed. To close the white space in the project plan, "marketing of technical services" was added as another horizontal stream.

Fast

How fast is fast? Rapid-results projects generally last no longer than 100 days. But they are by no means quick fixes, which imply shoddy or short-term solutions. And while they deliver quick wins, the more important value of these initiatives is that they change the way teams approach their work. The short time frame fosters a sense of personal challenge, ensuring that team members feel a sense of urgency right from the start that leaves no time to squander on big studies or interorganizational bickering. In traditional horizontal work streams, the gap between current status and the goal starts out far wider, and a feeling of urgency does not build up until a short time before the day of reckoning. Yet it is precisely at that point that committed teams kick into a high-creativity mode and begin to experiment with new ideas to get results. That kick comes right away in rapid-results initiatives.

A Shift in Accountability

In most complex projects, the executives shaping and assigning major work streams assume the vast majority of the responsibility for the project's success. They delegate execution risk to project teams, which are responsible for staying on time and on budget, but they inadvertently leave themselves carrying the full burden of white

THE WORLD BANK'S PROJECT PLAN

A project plan typically represents the planned activities as horizontal bars plotted over time. But in most cases, it's very difficult to accurately assess all the activities that will be required to complete a complicated long-term project. We don't know what will fall into the white space between the bars. It's also difficult to know whether these activities can be integrated seamlessly at the end; the teams working in isolation may develop solutions that won't fit together. Rapid-results initiatives cut across horizontal activities, focusing on a miniversion of the overall result rather than on a set of activities.

Here is a simplified version of the Nicaragua project described in this article. Each vertical team (depicted as a group by the vertical bar) includes representatives from every horizontal team, which makes the two types of initiatives mutually reinforcing. So, for example, the horizontal work stream labeled "Set up private-sector market in agricultural support services" includes activities like developing a system of coupons to subsidize farmers' purchases. The vertical team establishing service contracts between technical experts and farmers drew on this work, providing the farmers with coupons they could use to buy the technical services. This, in turn, drove competition in the private sector, calling on the work that the people on the horizontal training teams were doing—which led to better services.

RAPID-RESULTS PROJECT OBJECTIVES

Five rapid-results teams cut across the original five work streams, each focused on one specific objective:

Establish alternative feed.

Within 120 days, incorporate an alternative source for pig feed in 15 farms, and establish five purchase agreements.

Implement seed distribution.

Within 100 days, ensure that 80% of the enhanced corn seed is available to farmers.

Establish service contracts.

Within 100 days, secure commitments from private-sector experts to provide technical services to 150 farmers.

Increase milk production.

In 120 days, increase daily milk production from 600 to 1,600 gallons at 60 producers.

Increase animal weight and productivity.

In 100 days, increase pig weight by 30% and chicken productivity by 20% in 30 arms, using enhanced corn seed.

Overall project objective: Improve productivity of 120,000 farmers by 30% in 16 years

Long-term work streams

Reorganize government agricultural technical-service institutions

Set up private-sector market in agricultural support services

Strengthen National Institute for Agricultural Technology

Implement training programs for agricultural technical-service providers

Establish agricultural information management system

2000   2016

Rapid-results initiatives (drawing on the work of all long-term work streams)

space and integration risk. In World Bank projects, as in most complex and strategically critical efforts, these risks can be huge.

When executives assign a team responsibility for a result, however, the team is free—indeed, compelled—to find out what activities will be needed to produce the result and how those activities will fit together. This approach puts white space and integration risk onto the shoulders of the people doing the work. That's appropriate because, as they work, they can discover on the spot what's working and what's not. And in the end, they are rewarded not for performing a series of tasks but for delivering real value. Their success is correlated with benefits to the organization, which will come not only from implementing known activities but also from identifying and integrating new activities.

The milk productivity team in Nicaragua, for example, found out early on that the quantity of milk production was not the issue. The real problem was quality: Distributors were being forced to dump almost half the milk they had bought due to contamination, spoilage, and other problems. So the challenge was to produce milk acceptable to large distributors and manufacturers that complied with international quality standards. Based on this understanding, the team leader invited a representative of Parmalat, the biggest private company in Nicaragua's dairy sector, to join the team. Collaborating with this customer allowed the team to understand Parmalat's quality standards and thus introduce proper hygiene practices to the milk producers in Leon. The collaboration also identified the need for simple equipment such as a centrifuge that could test the quality of batches quickly.

The quality of milk improved steadily in the initial stage of the effort. But then the team discovered that its goal of tripling sales was in danger due to a logistics problem: There wasn't adequate storage available for the additional Grade A milk now being produced. Rather than invest in refrigeration facilities, the Parmalat team member (now assured of the quality of the milk) suggested that the company conduct collection runs in the area daily rather than twice weekly.

At the end of 120 days, the milk productivity team (renamed the "clean-milking" team) and the other four teams not only achieved their goals but also generated a new appreciation for the discovery process. As team leader Piccioni observed at a follow-up workshop: "I now realize how much of the overall success of the effort depends on people discovering for themselves what goals to set and what to do to achieve them."

What's more, the work is more rewarding for the people involved. It may seem paradoxical, but virtually all the teams we've encountered prefer to work on projects that have results-oriented goals, even though they involve some risk and require some discovery, rather than implement clearly predefined tasks.

The Leadership Balancing Act

Despite the obvious benefits of rapid-results initiatives, few companies should use them to replace the horizontal activities altogether. Because of their economies of scale, horizontal activities are a cost-efficient way to work. And so it is the job of the leadership team to balance rapid-results initiatives with longer-term horizontal activities, help spread insights from team to team, and blend everything into an overall implementation strategy.

In Nicaragua, the vertical teams drew members from the horizontal teams, but these people continued to work on the horizontal streams as well, and each team benefited from the work of the others. So, for example, when the milk productivity team discovered the need to educate farmers in clean-milking practices, the horizontal training team knew to adjust the design of its overall training programs accordingly.

The adhesive-material and office-product company Avery Dennison took a similar approach, creating a portfolio of rapid-results initiatives and horizontal work streams as the basis for its overall growth acceleration strategy. Just over a year ago, the company was engaged in various horizontal activities like new technology investments and market studies. The company was growing, but CEO Phil Neal and his leadership team were not satisfied with the pace. Although growth was a major corporate goal, the company had increased its revenues by only 8% in two years.

In August 2002, Neal and president Dean Scarborough tested the vertical approach in three North American divisions, launching 15 rapid-results teams in a matter of weeks. One was charged with securing one new order for an enhanced product, refined in collaboration with one large customer, within 100 days. Another focused on signing up three retail chains so it could use that experience to develop a methodology for moving into new distribution channels. A third aimed to book several hundred thousand dollars in sales in 100 days by providing—through a collaboration with three other suppliers—all the parts needed by a major customer. By December, it had become clear that the vertical growth initiatives were producing results, and the management team decided to extend the process throughout the company, supported by an extensive employee communication campaign. The horizontal activities continued, but at the same time dozens of teams, involving hundreds of people, started working on rapid-results initiatives. By the end of the first quarter of 2003, these teams yielded more than $8 million in new sales, and the company was forecasting that the initiatives would realize approximately $50 million in sales by the end of the year.

The Diversified Products business of Zurich North America, a division of Zurich Financial Services, has taken a similarly strategic approach. CEO Rob Fishman and chief underwriting officer Gary Kaplan commissioned and launched dozens of rapid-results initiatives between April 1999 and December 2002. Their overall long-term objectives were to improve their financial performance and strengthen relationships with core clients. And so they combined vertical teams focused on such goals as increasing payments from a small number of clients for value-added services with horizontal activities targeting staff training, internal processes, and the technology infrastructure. The results were dramatic: In less than four years, loss ratios in the property side of the business dropped by 90%, the expense ratio was cut in half, and fees for value-added services increased tenfold.

Now, when you're managing a portfolio of vertical initiatives and horizontal activities, one of the challenges becomes choosing where to focus the verticals. We generally advise company executives to identify aspects of the effort that they're fairly sure will fail if they are not closely coordinated with one another. We also engage the leadership team in a discussion aimed at identifying other areas of potential uncertainty or risk. Based on those discussions, we ask executives to think of projects that could replicate their longer-term goals on a small scale in a short time and provide the maximum opportunity for learning and discovery.

For instance, at Johnson & Johnson's pharmaceutical R&D group, Thomas Kirsch, the head of global quality assurance, needed to integrate the QA functions for two traditionally autonomous clinical R&D units whose people were located around the world. Full integration was a major undertaking that would unfold over many years, so in addition to launching an extensive series of horizontal activities like developing training standards and devising a system for standardizing currently disparate automated reports, Kirsch also assigned rapid-results teams to quickly put in place several standard operating procedures (SOPs) that cut across the horizontal work streams. The rapid-results teams were focused on the areas he perceived would put the company in the greatest danger of failing to comply with U.S. and European regulations and also on areas where he saw opportunities to generate knowledge that could be applied companywide. There's no science to this approach; it's an iterative process of successive approximation, not a cut-and-dried analytical exercise.

In fact, there are really no "wrong" choices when it comes to deciding which rapid-results initiatives to add to the portfolio. In the context of a large-scale, multiyear, high-stakes effort, each 100-day initiative focused on a targeted result is a relatively low-risk investment. Even if it does not fully realize its goal, the rapid-results initiative will produce valuable lessons and help further illuminate the path to the larger objective. And it will suggest other, and perhaps better-focused, targets for rapid results.

A Call for Humility

Rapid-results initiatives give some new responsibilities to frontline team members while challenging senior leaders to cede control and rethink the way they see themselves. Zurich North America's Gary Kaplan found that the process led him to reflect on his role. "I had to learn to let go: Establishing challenging goals and giving others the space to figure out what it takes to achieve these . . . did not come naturally to me."

Attempting to achieve complex goals in fast-moving and unpredictable environments is humbling. Few leaders and few organizations have figured out how to do it consistently. We believe that a starting point for greater success is shedding the blueprint model that has implicitly driven executive behavior in the management of major efforts. Managers expect they will be able to identify, plan for, and influence all the variables and players in advance, but they can't. Nobody is that smart or has that clear a crystal ball. They can, however, create an ongoing process of learning and discovery, challenging the people close to the action to produce results—and unleashing the organization's collective knowledge and creativity in pursuit of discovery and achievement.

Nadim F. Matta is Catalyst in Chief at the Rapid Results Institute. He was formerly managing partner at Schaffer Consulting. **Ronald N. Ashkenas** is a coauthor of the *Harvard Business Review Leader's Handbook* (Harvard Business Review Press, 2018) and a partner emeritus at Schaffer Consulting.

Maintaining Momentum and Overcoming Challenges

CHAPTER 14

Four Ways to Be More Effective at Execution

by Jack Zenger and Joseph Folkman

Most people recognize that execution is a critical skill and strive to perform it well, but they may (a) underestimate how important it is to their career advancement or (b) not realize that they can improve on execution without working longer hours.

On the first point, bosses place a premium on execution, which we define as the ability to achieve individual goals and objectives. In fact, when we asked senior managers to indicate the importance of this ability, they

---

Reprinted from hbr.org, originally published May 23, 2016 (product #H02WPK).

ranked it first on a list of 16 skills. Other raters in the organization ranked it fourth, behind inspiring and motivating, having integrity and honesty, and problem solving. We recognize that there are many parts of your job that are important, but if you want to move ahead in your career, it might be time to double down on simply getting more stuff done—it's what your boss wants to see.

Which brings us to the second point. Many managers react with defensiveness or despair to this news; after all, most of the managers we know already feel like they've got too much to do. People who are lethargic, slow, or unfocused are rarely (at least in our experience) promoted to upper-management positions. The leaders we know already work hard and long, and working harder and longer is not a viable option. In the short term, this typically yields improved results, but in the long term, leaders burn out. And if they've pushed their teams to do the same, team members quit.

But our data—gleaned from tens of thousands of 360-degree performance reviews—tells us that there are more sustainable methods of improving execution. We looked at thousands of leaders who were rated as being highly effective at execution and looked for the coinciding behaviors that enabled this skill. We found a set of behaviors that improve execution. Four behaviors in particular stood out.

Be Clear and Methodical

Many people who are energetic about execution tend to jump into activities and take action before they get organized, create a plan, or connect what they're doing to the strategy of the organization. Having the discipline to organize people, assemble resources, and then generate a plan that others can commit to will collectively improve execution. So will making clear who is doing what; we have learned that when everyone is collectively responsible, no one is responsible. Providing others with clear direction and a sense of connection to the strategy of the organization helps people understand how the work they are doing dovetails with the organization's mission.

If you are quick to jump into action and tend to start projects without a well-organized plan of attack, or if you get feedback on your lack of planning and organization, this suggestion might be one to focus on. An individual contributor might be able to get away with being disorganized, but it rarely works out well at the senior management level.

Set Stretch Goals and Deadlines

Setting stretch goals helps the group achieve its objectives and generates greater engagement and satisfaction in team members. To push the group to achieve those goals, pair them with deadlines. While we may not like it, when someone gives us a deadline, our behavior changes. Simply setting deadlines for goals and objectives goes a long way toward achieving those goals and objectives. If you resist setting stretch goals for your team, start by asking your team questions like, "What would it take to accomplish this goal two weeks earlier?" We find that by challenging your team and supporting them in accomplishing a difficult goal, team members actually feel more engaged and satisfied with their jobs.

But don't go overboard; we've also found that too much pushing can erode trust, which will hurt execution in the long run. When an untrusted leader asks for additional effort, people question their motives and resist their requests. Moreover, involving your team in the process of setting goals deadlines will increase their sense of commitment and autonomy.

Give More Feedback, Especially More Positive Feedback

Improve execution through intrinsic motivation, rather than through goals and deadlines. Leaders who are great executors are skilled at giving feedback. Specifically, the leaders who rate most highly are those who deliver critical feedback by taking the time to listen to and understand their employees' perspectives, rather than simply dropping a difficult message on someone and ending the conversation as quickly as possible.

But where we really saw a major difference was with *positive* feedback. Specifically, we found that leaders who are great at execution give a lot more positive recognition. Our research indicates that while giving a little more recognition did not affect execution, being above the 65th percentile on this skill had a major impact.

Resolve Conflict and Build Team Unity

Have you ever been part of a team so great that you love coming to work? Teams like this probably do all or most of the above—work assignments are clear and processes make sense, deadlines are ambitious but fair, and feedback is plentiful—but they also do something more. On these teams, it's not just the boss motivating team members; the expectations of peer team members are powerful motivators, too. Creating this kind of team culture is an important element of good execution. While there's a lot that goes into building high-performance teams, perhaps the biggest single thing for leaders to focus on is resolving conflict. That's because many of the problems within a team come from differences and conflict between team members; on high-performing teams, team members trust each other and conflict is constructive, not destructive or personal.

As you think about your ability to execute, all four of these dimensions are critical. You may focus on one or two and find that one is lacking. But our research shows that balancing all four of these factors is the strategy that will improve execution most of all.

Finally, if you've made it this far and you really feel as if you're already doing all of these things, and yet somehow you're still perceived as having an "execution problem," consider this: In our research, we also found that there's almost a one-to-one relationship between leaders who are seen as fast, and those who are seen as great executors. Previous work we've done has shown that some of the things we've discussed—setting stretch goals, having clear processes in place, and building trust, for example—will help you move faster. But you may also need to give your peers and bosses more evidence of your speed by, for example, being more transparent about how many projects you're working on and where they are in your pipeline.

———————

Jack Zenger is the CEO of Zenger/Folkman, a leadership development consultancy. Follow him on Twitter @jhzenger. **Joseph Folkman** is the president of Zenger/Folkman. Follow him on Twitter @joefolkman. They are coauthors of the book *Speed: How Leaders Accelerate Successful Execution.*

CHAPTER 15

Learning in the Thick of It

by Marilyn Darling, Charles Parry, and Joseph Moore

IDEA IN BRIEF

Like many managers, you probably conduct after-action reviews (AARs) to extract lessons from key projects and apply them to others. But in most companies, AARs don't fulfill their promise: Scrapped projects, poor investments, and failed safety measures repeat themselves, while hoped-for gains rarely materialize. One manufacturing executive, reading an AAR report for a failed

Adapted from an article in *Harvard Business Review*, July–August 2005 (product #R0507G).

project that had stumbled twice before, realized with horror that the team was "discovering" the same mistakes all over again.

How to transform your AARs from diagnoses of past failure into aids for future success? Realize that looking for lessons isn't the same as learning them. View the AAR as an ongoing learning process, rather than a onetime meeting, report, or postmortem. Set the stage for AARs with rigorous before-action planning—articulating your intended results, anticipated challenges, and lessons from previous similar situations. Conduct mini-AARs after each project milestone, holding everyone accountable for applying key lessons quickly in the next project phase.

Companies that master this process gain—and sustain—competitive advantage. They avoid repeating the kinds of errors that gnaw away at stakeholder value. And instead of merely fixing problems, they adapt more rapidly and effectively than rivals to challenges no one even imagined.

IDEA IN PRACTICE

To improve your AAR process:

Build your AAR regimen slowly

Rather than applying the AAR process across the board, begin using it selectively—on projects where the payoff is greatest and leaders have committed to working through several AAR cycles.

Focus on efforts critical to your team's mission, so people will be motivated to participate.

Conduct a before-action review (BAR)

Before embarking on an important project, answer these questions:

- **"What are our intended results and metrics?"**
  Does your team want to improve product quality?
  Accelerate its response to emergencies? Improve
  sales win/loss ratio?

- **"What challenges do we anticipate?"** Do you
  expect shortages of certain resources? A turn in
  customers' preferences?

- **"What have we or others learned from similar projects?"** Be candid about past failures—focusing on
  improving performance, not placing blame.

- **"What will enable us to succeed this time?"** What
  practices helped you succeed in earlier efforts?
  What worked before that should be tested under
  different circumstances?

Responses to these questions align team members' objectives and set the stage for effective AARs as your project unfolds.

Conduct mini-BARs and AARs

Break big projects into smaller chunks, bookended by short BAR and AAR meetings conducted in task-focused groups. You'll establish feedback loops that maximize project performance and foster an ongoing learning culture. But tailor your process to fit each project and project phase. For example, during periods of intense activity, use brief daily AAR meetings to help teams coordinate and improve the next day's work. At other times, less frequent meetings—monthly or quarterly—may be sufficient to identify and correct emerging problems.

Focus on your own team's learning

Lessons must first and foremost benefit your team, so resist any urge to create an AAR document specifically for some other corporate use. Focus team members on improving their own learning and, as a result, their own performance.

Your people may generate a lesson during the AAR process, but they won't have learned the lesson until they've changed their behavior. It takes multiple iterations to produce solutions that stand up under any conditions. (See the sidebar "Five Ways to Put AARs to Work at Work.")

———

Marilyn Darling, Charles Parry, and retired Colonel Joseph Moore were formerly researchers and consultants with Signet Consulting Group. Moore is a former commander of the 11th Armored Cavalry Regiment, the Opposing Force at the U.S. Army's National Training Center in Fort Irwin, California.

FIVE WAYS TO PUT AARS TO WORK AT WORK

The U.S. Army's standing enemy brigade (referred to as OPFOR) applies the after-action review (AAR) process to everything it does, but that's not realistic for most companies. Business leaders must act selectively, with an eye toward resources and potential payoffs. Don't even think about creating an AAR regimen without determining who is likely to learn from it and how they will benefit. Build slowly, beginning with activities where the payoff is greatest and where leaders have committed to working through several AAR cycles. Focus on areas critical to a team's mission so members have good reason to participate. And customize the process to fit each project and project phase. For example, during periods of intense activity, brief daily AAR meetings can help teams coordinate and improve the next day's activities. At other times, meetings might occur monthly or quarterly and be used to identify exceptions in volumes of operational data and to understand the causes. The level of activity should always match the potential value of lessons learned. Here are some ways you can use AARs, based on examples from companies that have used them effectively.

	The AAR in practice	The payoff
1 **Emergency response**	• Survey past emergencies to identify types of events and learning challenges. • Ask team members to take notes during the response process to facilitate the AAR.	• Avoid similar emergencies in the future. • Improve the speed and quality of your responses and damage control.

(continued)

FIVE WAYS TO PUT AARS TO WORK AT WORK

	The AAR in practice	The payoff
1 Emergency response (continued)	• Conduct AARs during the response process (if possible) or immediately afterward to begin building procedures and long-term solutions. • Periodically review past AARs to identify potential systems improvements.	• Improve the long-term effectiveness of your solutions.
2 Product dev	• Start each phase of product development with a before-action review (BAR). • Conduct AARs to identify insights to feed from one phase of product development into the next—and then into the next project. • Periodically conduct AARs on the product-planning process to identify potential improvements.	• Improve quality, reduce cost, and shorten time to market. • Anticipate customers' changing expectations.
3 Entering a new business or market	• Launch business planning with a BAR to reflect on past lessons. • Conduct AARs throughout the launch process to test lessons and create innovative solutions. • Conduct a wrap-up AAR to improve performance on the next venture.	• Apply lessons from past successes and failures to improve results on new ventures.
4 Sales	• Build AARs into the sales process, focusing as much on learning from wins as from losses. • Conduct AARs on customer defections to competitors' products.	• Improve the win/loss ratio. • Refine the value proposition for a new product.
5 Mergers and acquisitions	• Build AARs into strategy, negotiation, due diligence, and execution phases to continually reveal, test, and modify assumptions about the deal. • Wrap up each M&A activity by comparing it with previous efforts to identify problems and good ideas.	• Ensure that transactions deliver promised value to stakeholders.

CHAPTER 16

How to Hand Off an Innovation Project from One Team to Another

by Joe Brown

Companies invest millions in coming up with breakthrough innovations, but a sickening number of those investments fail. The truth is that you can have the right portfolio of investments, the right metrics and governance, the right stage-gate development process, and the right talent on the right teams, but if you don't design the right handoffs between your teams, all of that planning falls apart.

Adapted from content posted on hbr.org, August 23, 2018 (product #H04IGJ).

If innovation projects are going to succeed at scale in the marketplace, they'll need to survive a handoff from an innovation team to an execution team. And every time you create a handoff, you risk dropping the baton.

For example, one major Asian electronics company built a design lab to develop new hardware product ideas. All too often, when the design lab passed a concept on to a product manager, like a computer customized for 3D modelers and film editors, the PM would ignore the lab's thinking and simply apply the physical design of the computer to a product that she was already developing— like a low-powered computer targeted at students for the back-to-school season. When sales of the Frankenstein product missed their mark, everyone shared the blame. This electronics company had no clear plan for how projects would transition from the small design lab team back into the core business. It didn't have a handoff, it had a drop-off.

How do you prevent a drop-off? By tailoring each handoff to the teams involved. In many companies, innovation teams tend to fall into three buckets: "explorers," "scalers," and "optimizers" (with credit to Bud Caddell and Simon Wardley). Optimizers make up the core of most established businesses—they're skilled at enhancing and perfecting the existing business to drive growth or improve operations. Explorers work in teams like R&D, customer insights, or product development. Explorers are skilled at uncovering new opportunities in the face of ambiguity—they're people who translate inspiration into ideas using methods like design thinking. Scalers iteratively experiment and tweak new ideas until they find product-market fit using methods like agile or lean. These labels also nicely describe the phases of innovation: explore, scale, and optimize.

How should you create a smoother handoff between teams? There are four basic models for the handoff, and dozens of hybrids. The right one for each part of your innovation portfolio will depend on how integrated your projects need to be with your core business.

The Owner's Manual

This is both the most common handoff and the most difficult to pull off. After months—sometimes years— of work, an innovation team extensively documents its work in hundreds of pages of slides, spreadsheets, and other files, and then hands all of that over to a new team to execute. When was the last time you read an owner's manual? Exactly. You only pull out the owner's manual in a moment of panic when something is broken. In this model, a frightening amount of innovation work is skimmed over and forgotten. The new team then risks moving on without absorbing the learning of their predecessors. This model works best when there is no more ambiguity left in the challenge, when the project is ready for implementation by technical teams, and when the manual can be divided into small, specific, applicable chapters for each of its stakeholders.

The Architect

The best way to avoid a drop-off is to eliminate the handoff. In this model, the future owner of the work is embedded in the explorer and scaler teams. That person then acts as a connector, knowing all of the avenues already explored and all of the learning gained. This is a strong model for industries like consumer packaged goods, where one person, such as a brand manager, is responsible for product development from beginning to end. Although architects might not be leading the project in each phase, they will need to have final sign-off on the team's work. If the architects don't believe in the work, they'll end up killing the idea.

The Ambassadors

Similar to the previous model, in this model, members of the explorer, scaler, and optimizer teams remain embedded in each phase of the project to ensure that no learning is lost and that each phase of work is designed to feed smoothly into the next. In addition, this model improves the future work of innovation teams by helping them build an awareness of what downstream teams need most. This model is most common in software development teams, where UX designers may be involved in both early user research and long-term management of the product.

The Hive

In this model, multidisciplinary teams tackle challenges across the initiative's life cycle. This is most common in accelerators and incubators, where a new organization is set up as a microcosm of the parent company and made up of people from every major function and discipline. Hive teams also have representatives from functions that might normally act as corporate antibodies, like legal, finance, HR, or compliance. The hive pushes those protective functions from a posture of eliminating risk to one of reducing it—from saying no to saying "no, but . . . "

Other than the owner's manual, each of the other handoff models brings implementation teams along throughout the innovation process in order to seamlessly transfer knowledge. Doing this reduces the sense that a new idea was not invented here, and makes the handoff less like drinking from a firehose and more like a series of steady sips.

Joe Brown is a portfolio director at IDEO. Prior to IDEO, Brown taught courses in marketing and organizational behavior at Stanford Graduate School of Business, where he also earned his MBA.

CHAPTER 17

Making Process Improvements Stick

Research from Matthias Holweg, Bradley Staats, and David M. Upton

Starting with Frederick Taylor and W. Edwards Deming, managers have long been obsessed with ways to improve business processes. And in the past 20 years a host of improvement initiatives, including lean production, Six Sigma, and agile, have swept through a range of industries. Studies show that companies embracing such techniques may enjoy significant improvements in efficiency and costs. But when the University of North Carolina's

---

Reprinted from an article in *Harvard Business Review*, November–December 2018 (product #F1806A).

Brad Staats and the University of Oxford's Matthias Holweg and David Upton looked at the benefits, they noticed a gap. "These things always work well initially, but often the gains fade very quickly," Holweg says. "It's always felt like researchers were telling only half the story. It's not just about putting the programs in place—it's also about making them stick."

To understand why some improvements are sustained and others aren't, the researchers examined 204 lean projects launched from 2012 to 2017 at a European bank with more than 2,000 branches in 14 countries and serving more than 16 million customers. The lean initiative, started by the head office, was supported by a global consulting firm, which helped create an in-house academy to train lean "champions" at each regional subsidiary. Initial projects focused on processes (such as opening an account and making a wire transfer) that could benefit from decreased handoffs and fewer steps and were common to all regions. The regional offices subsequently identified additional projects according to their needs. The projects shared an overarching goal: to increase labor productivity, a key variable in service operations.

At first glance, the initiative appeared to be a great success. Over the first four years the bank launched 33 to 51 projects every six months, each involving 1,600 employees, on average. Initial improvements in efficiency averaged 10%; the gains rose to 20% after a year and 31% after two years. Those numbers are in line with the best-performing lean implementations in any industry, the researchers say, and the bank was rightly very pleased.

But when the researchers looked more closely, they found a more complicated picture. Despite the impressive aggregate gains, 21% of projects failed to yield any improvements. And among the 79% that showed initial improvements, many regressed: Only 73% were still producing results above baseline after a year, and after two years the number fell to 44%. Adding up the projects that had no improvements and the ones for which improvements were temporary, only slightly more than one-third of projects held on to gains after two years.

The researchers also explored whether projects that were initially successful could not only preserve the gains but also show continuous improvement—getting progressively better over time, which is the goal of many lean projects. Just 51% of them were continuing to improve a year after launch; after two years the figure dropped to 36%.

Seeking to understand these findings, the researchers looked at factors identified in previous research as influencing the initial success of lean projects: the experience of local leaders driving implementation, the level of training provided, and teams' familiarity in working together. None explained the difference, suggesting that what accounts for initial success is different from what's needed to hold on to gains or to improve further.

Interviews with lean champions in the bank's 14 countries provided some insight. Managers said that one condition needed to keep improving was visible support from board members and senior leadership—without it, frontline workers believe that the company's enthusiasm for the effort has waned, and backsliding ensues.

They also cited the need for consistent measurement and monitoring and noted that problems arise when significant early improvements give way to diminishing returns. "Addressing the low-hanging fruit is easy; it becomes harder in the long term," one lean champion told the researchers.

The data reinforces these observations. Projects with strong support from the head office showed 35% greater improvement after a year than ones without that support; they were also less likely to backslide, with 79% performing above baseline after a year, compared with 61% of projects not driven by the head office. "Senior leadership, through paying attention to the lean improvements, clearly has a major enabling role in sustaining improvements," the researchers write. Some companies hope that a continuous-improvement mentality will become embedded in their culture and will motivate frontline workers even without the involvement of senior leaders, but this work suggests that hope may be unrealistic.

The researchers also interviewed executives with deep experience leading lean initiatives across a range of industries; from this, they identified three ways in which organizations can help initiatives achieve sustained improvements.

The first is by communicating the program in a clear narrative that aligns with the organization's purpose. For example, a hotel might focus on how a lean process will improve guest satisfaction; that's more likely to motivate employees than an emphasis on cost savings. The second is by directing efforts toward pain points whose easing

IN PRACTICE: HELEN BEVAN

Helen Bevan has spent 25 years overseeing change initiatives at England's National Health Service, which serves more than 50 million patients and employs 1.2 million health care staffers. She spoke with HBR about the challenges of preserving the gains from one initiative while launching new efforts. Edited excerpts follow.

Why is it so hard to sustain an initiative's improvements?
It's an issue of energy. And when a new initiative comes along, people ask, "What do we do with the old one?" Much of our workforce models the behavior of senior leaders, and when those leaders shift their energy to something else, it's hard to sustain things.

What differentiates changes that stick?
Sustainability starts at the beginning, in how we frame a project and what it means to the organization and our purpose. It's the difference between behaving like a buyer and behaving like an investor. If we're asking doctors to get on board something that's underway, it's already too late. We need to get them invested in the project, and thinking like owners, well before it begins. When I look at the difference between projects that are sustained and ones that aren't, it often has to do with taking the time at the beginning to set them up, frame them the right way, and get people invested.

(continued)

IN PRACTICE: HELEN BEVAN

Is this especially hard in a health care setting, where efficiencies may seem to conflict with quality care?

Our purpose is health and wellness. That's what motivates people in this sector; they don't come for the pay. If we can frame a project as relating to things that really matter to the people who work here, they will connect with it on an emotional level. Even doctors, who make decisions logically, are more likely to engage and be motivated if an initiative fits with their emotions and values. So we show data and avoid jargon. If we talk about "lean" and "agile" and use words like *kanban, kaizen,* and *scrum,* it feels like we're taking away people's autonomy. We can convey those concepts perfectly well without those words.

But don't people worry that the programs are actually about cost cutting?

Of course we focus on costs—we have finite resources. But it's about framing. Instead of talking about waste, we focus on unwarranted variation in care. Every

would clearly benefit employees. For instance, one hospital's initiative aimed to decrease the time medical personnel spent on paperwork, freeing them up for patient care. The third is by ensuring that senior leaders act as coaches, enabling small wins to increase employees' motivation and engagement.

patient with the same condition should get the same high-quality treatment; when that doesn't happen, it can be a matter of life and death. Variation also adds to cost, so reducing unwarranted variation increases care and reduces cost. We see more success when we frame things in terms of our mission, which is care.

How do you start an initiative without losing the gains of the previous one?

Four years ago we did a crowdsourcing exercise in which we asked colleagues about the biggest barriers to change. The most common answer was "confusing strategies." People said that when a new initiative, target, goal, or focus comes along, they don't know whether it's more important than the previous one. We have to find ways to continue the journeys we've started by sustaining people's energy while creating space for new things. Managers and leaders must make sense of those things and reduce ambiguity.

A particularly troublesome obstacle to sustained improvement, the researchers say, is initiative fatigue, which occurs when leaders jump too quickly from one improvement fad to another. (One of the researchers has joked about the danger of airport bookstores, which tempt traveling executives to pick up business books that may send them in pursuit of a new improvement plan.) Embarking on a new project is often more exciting than staying the course, but that doesn't necessarily deliver the best long-term results. Staats says, "It's always easier to start something, whether it's weight loss, going to the gym, or smoking cessation. Getting individual changes to stick is hard, and getting organizational changes to stick is even harder." (See the sidebar "In Practice: Helen Bevan.")

———————

Matthias Holweg is the American Standard Companies Professor of Operations Management at Oxford University's Saïd Business School. **Bradley Staats** is an associate professor at the University of North Carolina's Kenan-Flagler Business School. **David M. Upton** was the American Standard Companies Professor of Operations Management at the University of Oxford's Saïd Business School.

CHAPTER 18

Your Initiative Needs an "Exit Champion"

by Isabelle Royer

You can still find them on eBay, sleek and gleaming videodisc players with LP-sized discs. The product: RCA's SelectaVision—one of the biggest consumer electronics flops of all time.

But it isn't simply the monumental failure in the marketplace that makes the SelectaVision story worth remembering. It's that RCA insisted on plowing money into the product long after all signs pointed to near certain failure. When the company developed its first

Adapted from "Why Bad Projects Are So Hard to Kill," *Harvard Business Review*, February 2013 (product #R0302C).

prototype in 1970, some experts already considered the phonograph-like technology obsolete. Seven years later, with the quality of VCRs improving and digital technology on the horizon, every one of RCA's competitors had abandoned videodisc research. Even in the face of tepid consumer response to SelectaVision's launch in 1981, RCA continued to develop new models and invest in production capacity. When the product was finally killed in 1984, it had cost the company an astounding $580 million and had tied up resources for 14 years.

Companies make similar mistakes—if on a somewhat more modest scale—all the time. "Why can't companies kill projects that are clearly doomed? Is it just poor management? Bureaucratic inertia? My research has uncovered something quite different. Hardly the product of managerial incompetence or entrenched bureaucracy, the failures I've examined resulted, ironically, from a fervent and widespread belief among managers in the inevitability of their projects' ultimate success. This sentiment typically originates, naturally enough, with a project's champion; it then spreads throughout the organization, often to the highest levels, reinforcing itself each step of the way. The result is what I call collective belief, and it can lead an otherwise rational organization into some very irrational behavior.

Of course, a strongly held conviction and the refusal to let inevitable setbacks undermine it are just what you need to get a project up and running. But there is a dark side: As the project moves forward, faith can blind you to increasingly negative feedback—from the lab, from vendors and partners, from customers.

My analysis revealed a number of practices that can help companies avoid this kind of disaster. For one, they can assemble project teams not entirely composed of people enthusiastically singing from the same hymnbook. They can put in place a well-defined review process—and then follow it. Perhaps most important, companies need to recognize the role of "exit champions": managers with the temperament and credibility to question the prevailing belief, demand hard data on the viability of the project, and, if necessary, forcefully make the case that it should be killed. While the importance of project champions is well documented, the value of someone who is able to pull the plug on a project before it becomes a money sink hasn't generally been appreciated.

Recognize the Role of the Exit Champion

Sometimes it takes an individual, rather than growing evidence, to shake the collective belief of a project team. If the problem with unbridled enthusiasm starts as an unintended consequence of the legitimate work of a project champion, then what may be needed is a countervailing force—an exit champion. These people are more than devil's advocates. Instead of simply raising questions about a project, they seek objective evidence showing that problems in fact exist. This allows them to challenge—or, given the ambiguity of existing data, conceivably even to confirm—the viability of a project. They then take action based on the data. At Essilor and Lafarge, two companies I studied for this article, exit

193

champions joined the projects as evidence of their un-promising futures was mounting. But supporters were still clinging to the shreds of positive evidence that oc-casionally emerged—or ignoring the evidence altogether. Had it not been for these exit champions, team members said later, the projects probably would have continued for months or even years.

To be effective, an exit champion needs to be directly involved in the project; a negative assessment from someone based elsewhere in the company is too easy to dismiss as ill-informed or motivated by organizational rivalry. The exit champion also needs a high degree of personal credibility. The exit champions at Essilor and Lafarge had been with their companies for a long time and were well regarded by top management. Both had a strong network of people at different levels of the com-pany ready to provide support when they decided the project should be killed.

What kind of person would willingly assume such a role? Even if killing a project doesn't put an exit cham-pion out of a job, the role, unlike that of a traditional project champion, seems to offer little in the way of pres-tige or other personal rewards. (For a discussion of the differences between the two roles, see the sidebar "The Exit Champion and the Project Champion.") In fact, the exit champion faces inevitable hostility from project sup-porters; those at Essilor and Lafarge were variously de-scribed as villains or dream breakers.

Consequently, exit champions need to be fearless, willing to put their reputations on the line and face

THE EXIT CHAMPION AND THE PROJECT CHAMPION

The types of individuals who gravitate toward the roles of project champion and exit champion are similar. Both must show initiative; after all, they have by definition assumed their roles rather than been assigned them. And they need to be energetic and determined enough to overcome the obstacles and inevitable skepticism they face. Given their similar personal traits, it's not surprising that, at a number of companies I studied, exit champions had been project champions at other points in their careers.

Differences between project champions and exit champions appear, however, in the particulars. For one thing, while project champions necessarily operate in an environment of uncertainty and ambiguity, exit champions need to remove ambiguity. They must gather hard data that will be convincing enough to overcome the opposition of believers. They need clear criteria for deciding whether to kill the project. When existing procedures don't include such criteria, they need to reach an agreement with believers on the criteria for assessing the new data; otherwise, reaching an agreement on the decision will be impossible. Thus, while project champions often violate procedures, exit champions typically have to introduce or restore them.

Project champions' reputations are often put at risk by their choice to champion what may turn out to be

(continued)

THE EXIT CHAMPION AND THE PROJECT CHAMPION

to be a failed project. Exit champions also put their reputations at risk, but the threat is of a different nature. Project champions run a long-term risk of being wrong—something that will become clear only if a project ultimately fails. Exit champions face the immediate risk that comes from challenging a popular project. That risk exists even if the exit champion is, in fact, ultimately right.

the likelihood of exclusion from the camaraderie of the project team. They need to be determined: Both Essilor's and Lafarge's exit champions failed in their first attempts to stop their projects. Perhaps most important, exit champions need to have some incentive for putting themselves out to halt a bad project. For many, this will simply be an acute distaste for wasted effort. As one exit champion at another company I researched said, "When I work, I need to believe in what I do. I don't want to waste time on something that is worthless."

It is important to understand that an exit champion is not a henchman sent by top management to kill the project. The exit champions at Essilor and Lafarge certainly weren't: They were assigned their positions only because their predecessors had left the company, and they simply took the initiative to determine if their projects were likely to be successful. Indeed, it wasn't initially clear to either of them that their respective projects *should* be killed. Although signs that the projects wouldn't succeed were accumulating, in neither case was the evidence conclusive because it wasn't based on hard data.

Senior executives need to recognize the exit champion as a defined role that someone might play in the organization—otherwise, they may not know exit champions for who they are and give them the support they will need. And they can take steps to create an environment in which such a savior would be more likely to emerge. Just as companies celebrate and recount stories of the great successes of product champions, they could perhaps identify and spread tales of courageous exit champions in their midst (or at other companies) who saved their organizations millions of dollars. Top managers should at the least make it clear that challenges to a popular project would be welcome or even rewarded. At the same time, though, they need to demand from the exit champion strong evidence of the project's weaknesses— just as they should have earlier demanded growing evidence of its viability.

Although they may not always be played out on such a grand scale as RCA's SelectaVision, stories like these are all too familiar in business. That's because belief is a powerful sentiment, and collective belief is even more powerful. Clearly, any project has to start with faith because there typically isn't much objective evidence, if any, at the beginning to justify it. But, as a project unfolds and investments increase, this faith has to be increasingly tested against the data. Indeed, the challenge for managers in the "can-do" culture of business is to distinguish between belief as a key driver of success— and belief as something that can blind managers to a project's ultimate failure.

———————

Isabelle Royer is a professor of strategy and management, specializing in decision making, at Université de Lyon Jean Moulin, iaelyon School of Management, Magellan.

Keeping Strategy and Execution Aligned

CHAPTER 19

Good Strategy Execution Requires Balancing Four Tensions

by Simon Horan and Michael Connerty

Putting strategy into practice is notoriously difficult. In our experience, the primary obstacle to strategy execution is a failure to balance the inherent tensions that characterize any major initiative. Successful strategy execution calls for skillful orchestration of sometimes opposing forces and competing needs. In particular, there are four core tensions that leaders need to balance.

Adapted from content posted on hbr.org, November 3, 2017 (product #H03YAX).

Tension #1: An Inspiring End State versus Challenging Targets

A vision of an inspirational "end state" is essential for getting people to commit to change: a simple narrative that articulates not only why change is necessary but also what life will look and feel like once change is successfully implemented.

However, aggressive "mid-state" targets are also required to provide direction and to challenge people to give their all. Among workers, an inspiring end state without challenging targets will likely elicit the response, "I will give this a go, and we can see where we land." That's not optimal. But at the same time, challenging targets without an inspiring end state leads to a grind in which workers often ask themselves, "Why am I doing this?"

Consider the experience of a major utility that made the strategic decision to undertake a broad-based initiative aimed at improving efficiency and reining in costs. When a detailed cost assessment identified significant savings potential, executive leadership boldly added another five percentage points to the target. The team tasked with overseeing the effort designed an aggressive implementation plan that tied targets to manager compensation. However, beyond the strategic goal of becoming an industry leader in terms of cost structure, there was no "story" for how this effort would complement the business's broader ambitions. After about six months, the effort began to falter, due primarily to staff frustration and a sense that the initiative lacked a compelling purpose.

Tension #2: Top-down Control versus Democratization of Change

When everyone in the organization feels empowered to make decisions that can influence change, it creates a palpable energy: People tend to work harder, offer more ideas, and become far more invested in the process. If every activity is the result of a command from on high, the company runs the risk of sucking all the energy out of the room. But the flip side can be myriad groups of enthusiastic change agents dashing off in multiple, un-coordinated directions.

The successful but challenging experience of a large pharmaceutical company illustrates the tension between top-down and decentralized change efforts. The company defined a new growth strategy that would require a significant improvement in its ability to innovate rapidly. While there was broad consensus on the strategy, there was disagreement within the leadership team regarding the best way to implement the strategy—especially when it came to making critical decisions, involving and empowering managers and staff, and holding people accountable for results. Tensions arose, and significant debate ensued over several months as the leadership team tried to work their way through an initial set of critical decisions that would guide execution. Ultimately, leadership managed to strike a balance across these areas, continuing to drive the change effort while soliciting contributions of a broad set of managers and staff. The result was a far stronger and more efficient R&D organization.

Tension #3: Capability Development versus Pressure for Results

Many strategies call for significant changes in the ways a company works, which raises questions of whether the organization needs to develop new capabilities. But the pressure to deliver immediate results is often so intense that an organization may be forced to forge ahead with its existing capabilities.

Take the example of a global industrial products company that was in the early stages of implementing a growth strategy. The strategy called for significant changes to the company's organizational structure and the way it marketed, sold, and serviced customers across numerous geographies. But as a publicly traded company, it was under the gun to deliver results every quarter. As the leadership team held numerous conversations across the organization about strategy execution, they came to the realization that most midlevel managers and frontline staff perceived serious capability gaps. This candid feedback allowed leadership to identify those capabilities most in need of strengthening in order for the strategy to be successful. At the same time, they were able to achieve some early wins that bought them time to develop these critical capabilities.

Tension #4: Creativity versus Discipline

Creativity is a part of any distinctive strategy. Fearing that discipline will stifle creativity, it is not uncommon for executives to choose to "let the creatives run free." At its best this can lead to unanticipated insights and outcomes, but at its worst it can lead to chaos and complete unaccountability for results. In fact, creativity and discipline are not mutually exclusive, yet this tension can be the hardest one to balance.

Consider the experience of a services business that had an iconic reputation for its one core service. Entering a new space had been elusive for many years, and in desperation the company gave the business development function complete freedom. It moved to a new building, changed its business cards, hired "disruptive thinkers," and experimented with all manner of innovation techniques. Several months (and several tons of Post-it notes) later, they were called in to report back, only to serve up a raft of tired ideas and zero outcomes.

Getting strategy done well often calls for trade-offs between delivering short-term results and implementing foundational changes that require time. Yet companies that can achieve a balance between opposing forces are far more likely to realize successful strategies that endure.

Simon Horan is a managing director at L.E.K. Consulting. **Michael Connerty** is a managing director in L.E.K. Consulting's Chicago office, where he helps lead the firm's organization and operations practices.

CHAPTER 20

Five Ways the Best Companies Close the Strategy-Execution Gap

by Michael Mankins

Executives say that they lose 40% of their strategy's potential value to breakdowns in execution. In our experience at Bain & Company, however, this strategy-to-performance gap is rarely the result of shortcomings in implementation; it is because the plans are flawed from the start.

Too many companies still follow a "plan-then-do" approach to strategy: The organization works tirelessly

---

Adapted from content posted on hbr.org, November 20, 2017 (product #H04OXD).

to create its best forecasts about the future market and competitive landscape. Leadership then specifies a plan that it believes will position the company to win in this predicted future. This approach may have made sense when first popularized by GE and others in the 1970s, but in today's fast-paced world, the "cone of uncertainty" surrounding future market and competitive conditions is too great for companies to prescribe every element of a multiyear strategy. The plan-then-do approach is obsolete, even dangerous.

Today's successful companies close the strategy-to-performance gap with a new strategy approach best described as "decide-do/refine-do." This agile, test-and-learn approach is better suited to today's tumultuous environment. It also helps bridge the chasms that exist at so many companies between great strategy, great execution, and great performance.

Here are five lessons we've gleaned from what we see the best companies doing.

Treat Strategy as Evergreen

The best companies see strategy less as a plan and more as a direction and agenda of decisions. In effect, a company's strategy is the sum of decisions it effectively makes and executes over time. This mindset focuses leadership on making near-term decisions with the longer-term destination in mind, but it doesn't presume that there is only one path from here to there.

Take Dell Technologies, for example. Following the company's go-private transaction in October 2013, Dell put in place new models for strategy development, resource allocation, and performance management. Instead of formulating detailed, long-term financial plans, executives at Dell now align around a common performance ambition—a cash flow vector consistent with growing the company's intrinsic value faster than competitors. Executives then delineate a multiyear outlook for each of Dell's businesses, capturing the current performance trajectory of the business given the decisions management has made to date. Finally, the team defines a strategy agenda comprising the highest value at stake and most urgent issues that leadership must address to close the gap between its ambition and Dell's current trajectory.

Dell's executive leadership team focuses on systematically addressing the issues on the company's strategy agenda. Once they address an issue and make a decision, they allocate the resources needed and turn to the next issue on the agenda. Strategy development at Dell is no longer a batch process tied to some planning calendar; it is a continuous process.

Value Flexibility

When the road is obstacle-free, the value of maneuverability is low. Leadership is better off selecting a single path forward, even if it limits the company's ability to steer around potential roadblocks. In today's world, however, flexibility matters.

The rise and fall of Webvan illustrates the cost of an inflexible strategy. Internet usage was growing fast when the world's first online grocery delivery business hit the scene in 1996. Webvan promised to deliver the best-quality groceries at the cheapest price by the click of a button. The strategy required a massive capital investment in a nationwide system of distribution centers with robotic stock-picking equipment. To justify the investment, Webvan made a bold forecast of future usage, order sizes, and costs. There were no reliable proxies to use to create this forecast. Any deviation from management's forecast meant failure, regardless of how effectively the strategy was executed. Unfortunately, usage turned out to be far lower than expected, order sizes much smaller, and capital costs far higher. Webvan was forced to cease operations by 2001.

Think of Strategy as a Portfolio of Options, Not Bonds

The traditional plan-then-do model treats the value of any strategy like a bond. Management forecasts the future coupon payments (or cash flows) associated with various strategies and then selects the one that has the highest discounted value. When volatility is high, however, strategic decisions should be treated more like call options. Leadership decides whether the small up-front investment is worth making as a call on potential profits. As long as the option appears "in the money," management can continue to invest; the moment the strategy becomes "out of the money," leadership can stop investing, cut its losses, and move on.

Take Google. Since 2005, Google (and more recently, its parent company, Alphabet) has invested in countless new ventures. Some have been highly publicized (YouTube, Nest, Google Glass, Motorola phones, Google

Fiber, self-driving cars); others are less well known (grocery delivery, photo sharing, online car insurance comparison). While many of the company's investments have succeeded, some have not. Larry Page and his team have been quick to respond, shedding these investments and doubling down on others. Over the past three years, Alphabet has closed smart home company Revolv, shut down Google Compare, paused Google Fiber, and sold Motorola Mobility to Lenovo. During this same period, the company has increased its stake in cloud services and various new undertakings managed by the company's X lab group. By treating strategic investments like options, Alphabet has avoided committing too early to new businesses. This approach has also allowed the company to double down on promising ventures and build them into profitable new businesses.

Create Response Mechanisms

In a world where the best-laid plans can go awry, companies that react quickly and effectively come out on top. Rigorous contingency planning is as important as disciplined action planning. It requires that you identify the most important known unknowns associated with your company's strategy, specify concrete steps to adjust course if you see an unplanned change in the external environment, and put in place mechanisms to continuously monitor market and competitive conditions. Caterpillar, for example, is reported to have put in place robust contingency plans in advance of the global financial crisis in 2007. Well before the crash, Caterpillar's CEO insisted that all division heads develop contingency plans for a recession. At the time, Caterpillar and its competitors were at full capacity, and global demand was high. Few of Caterpillar's competitors were contemplating a downturn. When the recession hit, Caterpillar put its contingency plans into effect, safeguarding the company's profits and giving it the ability to support critical players in the value chain.

Test and Learn, Then Test Some More

Agile planning can be thought of as a series of time-boxed sprints—or micro-battles, as my Bain colleague James Allen would say—with the objective of moving forward, testing the waters, learning, and refining the strategy based on the results.

Caesars Entertainment has built test-and-learn into its marketing investments. For gaming companies such as Caesars, promotions are a major strategic investment. Successful promotions (free hotel rooms, subsidized flights, comped meals) bring new customers to the casino, and the profits generated by the games they play offset the cost of the promotion. Many promotions are unsuccessful. Either they fail to spawn new customer interest or the cost of the promotion is too high relative to the incremental gains. Caesars uses its network of more than 50 casinos to test promotions before rolling them out. This test-and-learn approach lets Caesars limit the unsuccessful promotions and ensures that its most successful promotions are pushed out to as many casinos as possible.

Most companies do not take advantage of their opportunities to test and learn. They go for a big bang—

and risk a big bust—when a series of smaller, more productive bangs would generate better results.

Great performance requires great strategy *and* great execution, but poor execution is often used as an excuse for flawed strategy. Today's leaders need a new approach to strategy development. They can no longer define a plan over many years and then just do. Success requires identifying the next few steps along a broadly defined strategic path and then learning and refining as you go. This approach makes execution easier and increases the odds of delivering great results.

———————

Michael Mankins is a partner in Bain & Company's San Francisco office and a leader in the firm's Organization practice. He is a coauthor of *Time, Talent, Energy: Overcome Organizational Drag and Unleash Your Team's Productive Power* (Harvard Business Review Press, 2017).

CHAPTER 21

Your Strategy Has to Be Flexible— But So Does Your Execution

by Martin Reeves and Rodolphe Charme di Carlo

Peter Drucker said, "Plans are only good intentions unless they immediately degenerate into hard work." This and a slew of similar maxims reflect a common view of strategy execution: that it's distinct from strategy, harder to pull off than defining a strategy, and therefore more critical to success—underpinned by seemingly

Adapted from content posted on hbr.org, November 14, 2017 (product #H040FE).

indisputable virtues such as diligence, discipline, consistency, alignment, and focus. But such a simplistic view of execution can be misleading and can reduce actual impact.

In fact, several frequently observed traps result from such a view of execution:

Losing the plot

Action plans and Gantt charts can span many pages in pursuit of precision and concreteness. But excessive complexity can undermine thoughtful execution as much as a failure to specify tactics. In the worst case, busyness can become an implicit goal or cultural norm, and the original strategic intent can be lost in a frenzy of detail and activity. Execution must be insightfully focused on the most critical aspects of a challenge, or those which unlock other critical actions. For example, if category expansion is critical to value creation in a particular strategy, plans should focus disproportionally on how to achieve this. For example, former Mars' president Paul Michaels shares in *Your Strategy Needs a Strategy*: "The job of strategy for a segment leader like us is to drive category growth, and that's the thing you should be thinking about all the time."

Metric obsession

Drucker's exhortation "What gets measured gets managed" is often invoked when approaching execution. In the sense that results count, and their quantification is desirable, it seems irrefutable. But the worst way to achieve a goal can sometimes be to pursue it directly. For example, new drugs are not discovered by pursuing a target number of new drugs, but rather by exploring new areas of chemistry and biology. It is also a mistake to restrict ourselves to managing what we can easily measure. Few would deny the importance of corporate culture, for example, even though it is not easily quantifiable.

Planning myopia

Emphasizing compliance with a plan can, under stable conditions, accelerate fruition of a strategy. But under the changing conditions of a nascent or recently disrupted industry, a rigid plan can become a straitjacket for the flexibility and adaptation that are required to succeed. To take a historical example, centrally planned economies in the Eastern Bloc left no space for adaptation to even the simplest types of change, like variation in demand. This inevitably created shortages and oversupply of goods.

Missed learning opportunities

The value of execution can, in the simplest cases, be boiled down to the successful accomplishment of specific tasks. But where a high degree of uncertainty and change is involved, the value can instead reside in the learning that accompanies execution, whether or not the immediate outcome is successful. A famous example is YouTube, which began as a video dating site back in 2005. The site failed to gain traction, so the founders, leveraging what they learned while building the original platform, launched another version of the website focusing on sharing videos online, with significantly more success.

Tyranny of intermediate goals

When goals and tasks are broken down several times into lower-level ones, it can clarify what is required of an individual or department and can therefore help scale the job of execution. But often the intermediate goal or task becomes an end in itself. A famous example is Hoover's free flights promotion. In 1992, to free up warehouse space, the U.K. team promised free airline tickets to customers who purchased more than £100 worth of its products. A little later, the U.S. marketing team offered the same promotion to U.S. customers in order to boost sales. The offer was implemented so "successfully" that the company could meet neither the demand for vacuum cleaners, nor the cost of the flights. As a consequence, after the courts settled customer complaints, the U.S.-based company had lost £48 million and had to sell its U.K. branch a few years later.

Missing the forest for the trees

Strategic plans are often broken down into different modules for execution by different parts of an organization. Yet sometimes optimization of the parts does not lead to optimization of the whole. To take a biological example, the U.S. National Parks policy used to be to extinguish all forest fires. This led to an increase in the severity of fires. Why? Because most fires are small and stop by themselves, while creating natural firebreaks and eliminating the undergrowth that can fuel larger fires. In 1972, the policy was therefore adjusted so that only man-made fires were fought. Businesses can be equally complex: A diversity initiative, for example, might include some compulsory training, but if this triggers sentiments of resistance and skepticism, it can be self-defeating. Every action can change perceptions, motivations, and actions, such that a list of individually plausible actions can easily create the opposite of the intended effect. In such cases, a holistic perspective to strategy and execution is required.

Execution as a thing

We often treat strategy and execution as being separable disciplines, each with its own distinct and constant character. But as we have shown in *Your Strategy Needs a Strategy*, different strategic environments require different approaches to strategy and execution. A nascent technology business might require an adaptive approach, and a stable commodity business might require a classical, planning-based approach. In predictable classical environments, strategy formulation can be separated from execution. But in adaptive environments, it cannot, since strategy continually emerges from amplifying the results of success experiments, that is, execution. Furthermore, the nature of execution is also very different for each case. In the first, it centers on compliance to a predetermined plan, in the latter on decentralized initiative taking and experimentation.

Tyranny of practicality

That an execution plan be "practical"—simple, concrete, familiar, and unchanging—seems incontrovertible. Execution is praxis, after all. But when dealing with new or changing situations, familiar, plausible actions can easily fail to achieve the desired effect. Polaroid, for example, was a pioneer in digital photography. Yet, it tried to sell its digital cameras using the same business model as its film-based cameras—by aiming to make high margins on instant film sales. Believing that users would want hard copies, it added digital technology to instant cameras, instead of creating a new product not requiring film. As we now know, the company lost to rivals. Former Polaroid CEO DiCamillo summarizes the company's failure well: "The reason we couldn't stop the engine was that instant film was the core of the financial model of this company." More broadly, a mature business can often create its own increasingly questionable reality by focusing on the part of the market where its own beliefs about how things work still apply, creating a double opportunity for disrupters—one physical and one mental. Indeed, entrepreneurs and disrupters often refer to this double inertia of incumbents as their greatest asset in taking on incumbents.

We should not let the simplistic but comforting dualism of strategy and execution deceive us. Execution should be as varied, thoughtful, subtle, diverse, and intertwined with strategy as is necessary to get the job done, and that will vary according to the specific challenge at hand. In short, your execution needs a strategy.

Martin Reeves is a senior partner and managing director in the Boston Consulting Group's New York office and the director of the BCG Henderson Institute. He is the coauthor of *Your Strategy Needs a Strategy* (Harvard Business Review Press, 2015). Follow him on Twitter @MartinKReeves. **Rodolphe Charme di Carlo** is a principal in the Boston Consulting Group's Dubai office.

Index

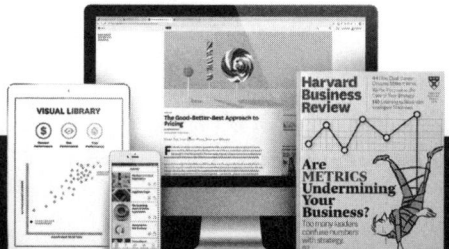

Smart advice and inspiration from a source you trust.

If you enjoyed this book and want more comprehensive guidance on essential professional skills, turn to the HBR Guides Boxed Set. Packed with the practical advice you need to succeed, this seven-volume collection provides smart answers to your most pressing work challenges, from writing more effective emails and delivering persuasive presentations to selling priorities and managing up and across.

Harvard Business Review Guides

Available in paperback or ebook format. Plus, find downloadable tools and templates to help you get started.

- Better Business Writing
- Building Your Business Case
- Buying a Small Business
- Coaching Employees
- Delivering Effective Feedback
- Finance Basics for Managers
- Getting the Mentoring You Need
- Getting the Right Work Done

- Leading Teams
- Making Every Meeting Matter
- Managing Stress at Work
- Managing Up and Across
- Negotiating
- Office Politics
- Persuasive Presentations
- Project Management

Notes

Notes

Notes

Notes